To: Jo[s]
with gr[ ]
for your endorsement
and encouragement —

Louise Sedgwick

Lifted
from
Shame
Trauma to Redemption

Louise Sedgwick

Lifted from Shame: Trauma to Redemption
Copyright © 2022 by Louise Sedgwick
Author website: www.louisesedgwick.com
BookBaby, 7905 N. Crescent Blvd, Pennsauken Township, NJ 08110

ISBN (Print Edition): 978-1-66786-697-0
ISBN (eBook Edition): 978-1-66786-698-7

All Scripture quotations, unless otherwise indicated, are taken from
THE HOLY BIBLE, NEW INTERNATIONAL VERSION®,
NIV® Copyright © 1973, 1978, 1984, 2011 by Biblica, Inc.®
Used by permission. All rights reserved worldwide.

Scripture quotations marked (TLB) are taken from *The Living Bible*,
copyright © 1971 by Tyndale House Foundation. Used by permission
of Tyndale House Publishers, Carol Stream, Illinois 60188. All
rights reserved. The Living Bible, TLB, and the The Living Bible
logo are registered trademarks of Tyndale House Publishers.

All Scripture quotations marked (KJV) are taken
from the King James Version. Public domain.

Some names and identifying details have been
changed to protect the privacy of individuals.

Editor: Jenne Acevedo, Acevedo Word Solutions LLC

Printed in the United States of America

Endorsements

"Jesus is the relentless inviter. He says to us, 'Come!' This spirit is in Louise Sedgwick's book, *Lifted from Shame*, as she invites you into her profound and miraculous story of redemption from trauma. With openhanded transparency, Louise moves us from her indescribable childhood sexual abuse to the long deliberate process of healing by her beloved Savior, whose voice of invitation she heard. 'Come, Louise! Come into places of wisdom and understanding. Come into the supernatural experience of grace. Come and exchange shame for hope. Come and recognize the power of the love of God.' Have you given up? Open this book. There is an invitation for you here to join Louise on the path to deliverance from all your fears."

—Dr. Kit Danley, president and founder,
Neighborhood Ministries, Phoenix, AZ

"I have underlined, starred, circled, and written notes throughout the pages of this story as the truths of God's grace and mercy hit me like waves again and again. Louise has shared a story of theology meeting our reality that is both truthful in the ongoing work of redemption and in the undoing of the effects of shame over years. It shows the beauty of God as a pursuer of persons and who is patient yet persistent to keep healing and bringing hope through His presence and the presence of community. Louise gives us a picture of the path God is taking us on in the working out of our salvation. We no longer have to try to figure out what we are supposed to do for God, but we are able to trust God with his destiny for our lives."

—Michael Acock, lead pastor,
Christian Fellowship of Columbia, MO

"Louise graciously and bravely pulls back the curtain of her life and deeply ministers to us through her story. The healing from childhood trauma and shame wasn't enough. It was only the first step of a process of reclaiming her identity and excavating the purposes God planned for her before the beginning of time. You may or may not identify with her trauma, but I imagine you will identify with the long, slow, and steady plan of God's sanctifying heart for our maturity. I'm reminded of Psalm 138:8. 'The LORD will fulfill his purpose for me; your steadfast love, O LORD, endures forever. Do not forsake the work of your hands.'"

—Sue Tell, architect and writer at *Echoes of Grace*, suetell.com; Navigators staff

"This is *not* a self-help book to improve a certain area of your life or curb a nagging habit, because in *Lifted from Shame: Trauma to Redemption*, Louise refuses to settle for anything resembling a quick fix. Based on her own life experience and testimony, she cuts down far deeper than many are willing to cut. But in doing she reveals both the abyss of human shame and yet the far deeper chasm of God's mercy and grace. The end result is an invitation to trust—to trust not simply on an intellectual level, but to trust in an integrated, life-changing kind of way."

—Joshua Rutledge, Vice President of Spiritual Development, Liberty University

For Norma

Table of Contents

Introduction

I trusted no one. Not a soul. Not friends, not family, not anyone in authority, and definitely not God. I wanted to believe I could trust myself, but even that was questionable. How could there be trust after what happened? My abuser told me he loved me before he violated me. And God, the sovereign creator of the universe, the One who claims to be love itself, allowed it to happen.

The abuse happened my entire childhood. I blamed myself for the harm I experienced, believing if I were stronger or more clever I would have found a way to avoid it. It must have been my fault that it continued.

Besides the self-contempt for my inability to create an escape route, I held a dark conviction in my mind that I deserved what happened. Only someone as deficient as me would be exploited as I was. I wasn't worth protecting and loving. If my abuser continued to mistreat me, and God permitted it to happen, how was I to believe anyone else might find something in me to value?

As a child I began to hide and pretend so the shame I believed defined me would not be discovered by others. Hiding in plain sight was preferable to rejection. I had a tremendous fear of being known. If anyone came too close, they might detect what I attempted to mask. I believed I was less than, undesirable, unlovely, unlovable, and unworthy of respect. I needed to disguise myself.

The Distortion of Shame

Destructive shame ruled my life, but I didn't know it. I viewed myself and the world through the distortion of shame. Even though I asked Jesus to be my Savior as a young girl, my struggle of contemptuous self-evaluation lingered. I carried the destruction into my adult life without relief or healing.

I thought I was the only one whose opinion of self was low. I have since learned that shame is a universal experience. People the world over have sustained relational hurt that induces a message of self-blame. Others feel shame for behaviors they can't control. Shame is born through a variety of life troubles and always produces the same result: judgment toward self and others.

No Helpful Answers

Even amid foundational Christian truths I had learned, no helpful answers were given for my questions. How was I to experience the victorious life I kept hearing about? It felt elusive to me. How could I be free of the heaviness in my heart? How could I stop hurting myself or others by my shame-fueled criticism? I was instructed to work harder and trust God. This is a sincere problem for us believers who have tried with all our might and keep failing. For those of us with an issue with trust, it appears insurmountable. Scriptures quoted seem out of reach. Encouragements in the faith resound like cliches.

Questions arose out of the pain of the abuse. Where is God when sin's destruction overwhelms? Was He there and did He care when the injury happened? Does He care in the aftermath of the anguish? What does one do with the shame of the sin? Is there a way out of feeling worthless? Is it possible to trust God or anyone else after relational betrayal?

Nothing feels more like reinjury to someone deeply harmed by sin than when platitudes of the goodness of God are shared without understanding or empathy for what the person has experienced. Sin creates complex effects in us that can make truth confusing. People who have experienced deep relational hurts need a safe place to process the pain. They also need authentic answers that offer healing and hope.

Trauma Research

In recent decades careful research has revealed the effects of trauma on the brain. The discovery of the physiological and psychological impact of trauma is exciting and encouraging for the survivors of it and those who love them. This research reveals that the effects survivors feel from the harm are real. Validation that we are not alone in our experience is heartening. Treatments for these effects have changed lives as the brain experiences healing.

These giant steps in the care of those who have suffered great harm are worthy of celebration. I encourage trauma survivors to consider these treatments by qualified professionals. However, this book's focus is the healing of the soul. Trauma scars the mind as well as the soul. Both parts of the human experience of trauma need healing.

Journey to Healing

Lifted from Shame shares my journey to this soul healing. It doesn't give formulas. It gives hope and tools to aid in growth toward trust along the way. Healing of the shame that arises from deep relational hurts and our own foolish choices takes time and is messy—but is realizable. With God, all things are possible. His grace and truth set us free.

Together we will look at the past and understand how shame is born. We will see how shame manifests in us, affecting families, work, and our relationship with God. We will explore the reasons behind our self-protective behaviors. And we will begin the journey of healing.

You will witness the slow but steady process of my healing from shame and the journey as I began to trust someone for the first time in my life. The heaviness of the pain of shame lifts to glory as God does His healing work. You will read of the transformation from performance to grace, from bitterness to joy, from fear to trust, and from despair to hope.

The miracle of healing is worthy of celebration on its own. However, the beauty of the story isn't just in the healing from the woundedness of the past. It is in the power of the redemption of that story for God's glory and our joy. The truths I learned, the practical tools I used, the Scripture that became real, the insights about sin and shame gleaned, and the love experienced weren't for me alone. They were to be passed on to others. To you.

Coming Alongside Others

The same environment where I healed, a church full of ragamuffins like me, became the place where, in great measure, I lived out the redemption of my story. For twenty-two years I was on the pastoral staff at this church, and I was privileged to walk with scores of my brothers and sisters in Christ on their journeys to trust God and others. I witnessed the power of the cross and the power of the resurrection change lives over and over again. This same transforming power that healed me and others is available to you.

Join me on a journey to understand shame and walk toward His promised hope. Isaiah 61:7 says, "Instead of their shame my people will receive a double portion, and instead of disgrace they will rejoice in their inheritance; and so they will inherit a double portion in their land, and everlasting joy will be theirs." Jesus and His grace set us free from the bondage to shame. He is able. He is willing. He longs for you to turn your face toward Him. He understands the betrayal and confusion that keep you from trusting Him. He will not fail you. He is faithful. He loves and values you more than you may understand today. If God can do it for me, He can do it for you. There is hope.

Chapter 1

BIRTH OF SHAME

If you didn't get too close, we looked fairly good from the outside. Our family of six—mom, dad, three girls, and a boy—lived in a middle-class neighborhood in a Midwestern city with sloping hills and lush green grass. Almost everyone in the community went to church and were conservative upright citizens. My siblings and I performed well in school, receiving high marks in academics and good reports on our behavior. My father was a respected Bible teacher, and my mother played the piano and organ in the churches we attended. We were clean and had food to eat and clothes to wear. It looked right and good, but what went on behind closed doors was quite the opposite.

This hidden reality didn't come out of nowhere. The trail of unaddressed sin in my family was generations long. According to my father's brother, their dad was a violent alcoholic who beat his wife and sons "to a bloody pulp" almost every day of their lives. In those days, there wasn't help available for families where abuse reigns. My grandmother did what she knew to do, sometimes leaving her husband, filing for divorce, then deciding against it. When the boys' behavior became out of control, she returned to him. She told me once she didn't know what else to do. "The boys needed their father," she explained. My father's upbringing was fraught with chaos, physical abuse, and pain. His significant unresolved wounding spilled over onto us.

My mother's parents were loving and safe, but her father was not what my mother needed him to be. Though he was faithful and stable, he was absent, spending his nights at the Masonic Lodge or doing side plumbing jobs. This took priority over building a relationship with his daughter. They were surrounded in the neighborhood by aunts, uncles, and cousins, but the lack of deep connection with her father left a dangerous and empty hole for my mother.

Fear and Powerlessness

My parents married young and had all four kids within eight years of their wedding. In our home, confusion, fear, and abuse reigned. We had moments of laughter and happy memories, but a lingering darkness overshadowed them. I never knew what to expect from my father. Was he in a good mood, or did I have to be careful of my every word and action? I waited to hear how the car door closed when he came home from work. On a good day the door clicked shut, and I could relax. But if it slammed, *watch out*. When his mood was foul, my heart raced and hypervigilance set in, gearing up for what I might experience at his hand.

Sometimes this moodiness looked like rage, and sometimes it appeared as childish pouting. Other times we heard about the faults of the pastor at church or what was wrong with the politician in office. My father ruled over everything we did and said. He maintained complete control of what we wore, having to approve all clothing as modest in his eyes, giving inspections before we headed out the door. He believed everything could be lumped into categories of right or wrong and pressured us to live by those convictions. I had no choice, no voice, and no room for my own ideas.

Steeped in doctrine and Scripture, my father twisted them as tools of manipulation and abuse. We dressed as we did because the Bible said so. We stood politically as we did because that is what Christians do. Christians didn't smoke, drink, dance, or disobey their parents. Any infraction gave my father liberty, in his view, to step in and correct us. He gave himself permission to punish in the way he wanted because he was the head of the home. Submission and obedience were the mandate. We were powerless to stand against him, though I made vain attempts to do so.

My father told me he loved me right after he abused me. How confusing is that mixed message for a child? I believed I deserved the abuse because he told me so using Scripture. "Children, obey your parents *in all things*," he quoted from Colossians 3:20 KJV (emphasis mine). What was I to do but take what he did as just punishment for my sin? It must have been my fault.

I feared my father and the powerlessness of life with him. I longed for his approval and real love but felt repulsed by his touch and his kisses. I hated him and wanted to stay as far away from him as possible but didn't know how to escape or where to run. Once as a grade schooler, I packed a bag and ran out the door. I didn't know where to go. I had less than a dollar in my Barbie wallet and all the clothes I owned in my Mary Poppins bag. I didn't know where to find a phone and didn't have a number to call. I stood at the street corner, feeling helpless and hopeless. After a time, I sighed and returned home. My father's sinister grin greeted me when our eyes met as I walked through the door.

Shame in Me

I didn't have a word for it then, but I felt it every day. *Shame.* Embarrassed that this was my family—and these were my parents. I was their offspring. I had the same last name, the same address, and the same brown wavy hair. I carried their shame within my very person.

I trusted no one. It was stressful to carry the shame for what my friends saw, but I also carried the shame of what they didn't see. I couldn't trust my father. I didn't trust my mother. Where could I turn? I made a vow with myself as a young teenager to do whatever it took for the rest of my life to never make a mistake and never trust anyone. I believed living in this way would keep me safe from harm and exposure, though it instead made me unsafe. It was an impossible vow to keep.

Because danger lurked at every turn, fear reigned. Anger was ever present in me and, though I used it as a weapon of defense, it felt more powerful than me. Scripture said I was not to fear and that rage was sin. These truths penetrated my heart. My fear and anger gnawed at me. They exposed I was not the obedient and sweet Christian woman I wanted to be.

Kingdom Purposes

I asked Jesus to come into my heart when I was a little girl. My parents raised us in churches that preached the gospel. My earliest happy memories are from when I attended church and learned about God and His love for me. I was wooed to the heart of God through being honored in my church. Investing in the spiritual lives of children in age-appropriate ways was a priority there. I heard that Jesus loved me enough to die for my sins so if I believed in Him, I could go to heaven and be with Him when I die. I received these truths without hesitation, and when I was four years old, I sat on the hill in front of my house and asked Jesus to forgive my sins and come into my heart. At the time, I had no idea how this decision would protect me from what I was to endure for the rest of my childhood. God heard me and washed my heart clean and came to dwell in my heart by the Holy Spirit, just as I asked Him to do.

The joy of my newfound faith didn't last long. Living with parents who twisted Scripture as the guide for what was said and done made me embarrassed to be a Christian. I associated Christianity with my father's eccentric and hurtful behaviors, and I wanted no part of it.

Everything changed at junior high church camp. The teaching of two men who loved Jesus and loved kids was used by God to change the direction of my life. Up until that point, I hadn't understood that the Christian life was about an ongoing, trusting, personal relationship with Jesus. I thought it meant compliant behavior to a distant, harsh, and uncaring deity. The Holy Spirit was at work in me that week in powerful ways. Tears streamed down my face as I prayed, "God, I am Yours. I dedicate my life to You fully. Use me big for Your kingdom purposes. I no longer want to be ashamed to be a Christian. I want to lift up Your name. Do with me as You wish."

To this day, I define my life as before this commitment and after. No longer was going to church about hanging out with my friends and trying to win every Bible drill or Scripture memorization contest so I could earn candy or a prize. It was about worshiping the One who had given His life for me and learning what He had for me. I chose a life verse from my King James Bible: "I will declare thy name unto my brethren: in the midst of the congregation will I praise thee" (Ps. 22:22).

In the following months and years, I felt an urgency to speak forth what Jesus did for us. I wanted to declare who God is so everyone could know. I shared the gospel with my friends in school. I studied my Bible and prayed often throughout each day. Jesus became the central and driving force of my life. I wanted to please God and know Him. My frantic efforts of performance were all I knew to attain this.

Performance in Me

I felt tremendous guilt and grief over my sin that continued to spiral out of control. I was angry, judgmental, and critical. I was full of shame, felt ugly and worthless, yet I struggled with pride. I evaluated everyone and found endless routes to superiority. I discerned what others should be doing and identified what they didn't do that I did. I longed to be loving and gracious like Jesus but had no idea how to stop criticizing and choose kindness. Nothing I did to improve my behavior worked. I felt like a failure as a Christian and deemed myself unworthy of God's love.

In the churches my family attended, I was taught powerful truths about God and His Word. Not all, but some principles I learned produced fear and performance in me. I was taught I needed God's grace for my salvation, but after that, my growth in Christ was up to me. I needed to strive to be all God created me to be. Leaders instructed us to consecrate ourselves to God and sin as little as possible. They said the less I sinned, the more others might want to be a Christian like me. Because I had given my life to Jesus, this is what I longed to do.

The problem with this strategy was that I couldn't keep it up. I always fell short. I might get "on fire for God" after camp or a youth rally, but then my zeal petered out and my criticism of others returned. My anger exploded. I didn't want to forgive those who hurt me. I gossiped often. I felt my heart become bitter. Something wasn't working, and I was sure the problem was me.

My struggle with anger grew in my teen years. God saw the strife within me and gave a great gift to sustain me in that season. While a high school student, a sacrificial young couple invested in the teenagers of our church. The wife met with me weekly to disciple me, encouraging me to build my life foundations on God's Word and His truth. We memorized Romans 6–8 together. We talked about prayer and the importance of a daily routine of reading God's Word. In our meetings she gave me permission to share some of my life struggles.

I didn't have courage to share my family dynamics with her, but I told her about my battle with rage. I asked her how I could stop being so angry all the time. She did the best she could, responding in kindness and grace. She quoted, "Thy word have I hid in mine heart, that I might not sin against thee" (Ps. 119:11 KJV). She encouraged me to go through Scripture and write down every verse on anger I could find. When I felt anger coming on, she prompted me to quote Scripture instead. For five years I carried a little spiral notebook in my purse with verses on each page. I followed her directions—and nothing changed. My anger didn't diminish. It increased as I felt the hopelessness of being entrapped in a behavior that was more powerful than me.

A New Environment

I went away to college after high school graduation, thankful to be far away from home. I felt safer. College was a different environment, yet I found I couldn't control my emotions. My anger lingered at the surface. My fury wasn't about my parents as I thought of them. It was anger that boiled over when life didn't go my way. I overreacted to my floormates and needed to keep myself in check. If I didn't, I exploded at the slightest affront.

I met my future husband, Chuck, while at college. Our dating life was painful and rocky. Well-meaning friends encouraged me to break up with him. They saw the distress of what we both endured in our relationship. The conflict I had with Chuck along with my rage issues exposed the reality of my brokenness. My shame increased.

In the summer of 1979, I was twenty-two years old and living in a rental house with four girlfriends. My cynicism about the Christian life intensified. I felt miserable, without peace or joy in Christ. I was filled with anger, bitterness, discouragement, and discontentment. I had it out with God one day as I sat on my bed. I prayed, "God, it seems to me that all I have been taught thus far about you and the Christian life is a crock. I've been taught that Christians can have victory over sin. I don't believe it. As far as it has to do with my rage and the sins I'm trying to control, it seems to me that I'm the one doing all the work. In my opinion, if there is victory over sin for a Christian, there has to be something supernatural involved. *You* have to do something about my sin. God, I don't know anyone who can give me answers. If there is a place that can teach me a different way, will you please take me there?" I heard no response. Out of fear of God's wrath and a hidden hope that perhaps there was another way, I continued to follow Jesus.

I came to realize I had an expectation that if I lived apart from my parents, my shame would lift and my anger fade. I discovered that the geographic change didn't bring an improvement to my struggle. The pain and guilt came with me wherever I went. My hopelessness to be free of the shame and the bondage to anger and judgmental criticism multiplied. What did I need? A good job to make me feel fulfilled? A great apartment? More ministry to make God happy with me? Nothing seemed to work.

New Family and Church

In the next ten years, Chuck and I married and had two daughters. The rage, superiority, and driven perfectionism that, in some ways, defined my life nearly destroyed my marriage and family. The shame I carried into my adult life heightened when, in my perception, my young husband's behavior and responses to me revealed my unworthiness to be loved and cherished. I lived in utter hopelessness that my relational needs would ever be met, that I would feel acceptable and safe, or that I would be able to love and honor him or my children well.

In June 1989, we started attending a new church and I joined a 12-step support group they offered. There I began what I later learned to be my healing journey. In this 12-step group, I learned about family systems, frozen feelings, people pleasing, control dynamics, no-talk rules, fear of trusting, and shame. I learned that coming to the end of yourself and admitting you can't manage your life is a step toward health and maturity. I learned I needed to let go of trying to control my life and let

God do the work in me. I experienced unconditional love and acceptance in this group and began working the 12 Steps. I began to discern how my childhood affected me and that I needed to take responsibility for my destructive behavior. I couldn't blame my parents for what I did today because of what they had done to me. I began to have hope. Maybe God could heal me and I could live in a healthier way.

While I attended this group, our wise and gentle-hearted leader, Nancy, called me a few weeks into the process. She invited me to start meeting with Rick, the senior pastor of our church. I agreed to call him. I was desperate for answers to what I couldn't understand about God and about my life.

I pursued other spiritual leaders through the years who I thought might be able to help me. I'd tell those leaders that I hated my parents, and each time they responded in the same way. "All parents make mistakes. You will understand more as you grow older and have your own children."

This was not my experience with Rick. As I sat in the chair across his desk, he asked what brought me to him.

"I hate my parents," I answered.

He leaned in a little bit and asked, "Why?"

His question unsettled me in the right way. Merely asking the question validated there might be a reason for such bitterness and contempt.

Being Understood

In the year that followed, Rick listened and asked questions about my childhood experience and about the current state of my life and heart. He helped me understand the nature of sin and how it affects all of us. He helped me understand the legalism from my childhood and the shame story I carried. He spoke with gentleness and compassion, understanding and wisdom. He wasn't overwhelmed by my intensity or brokenness. He cared for me as a good shepherd would. Instead of running away or dismissing me, he came toward me. He could do this because of his confidence in what Jesus had accomplished for me on the cross and at His resurrection. His faith and hope in what God could do to heal me began to bring light into the darkness I carried in my soul.

My pastor explained Scripture to me, taking me through Romans 6–8, the very chapters my caring high school leader asked me to memorize years before. This time I read the chapters with new understanding. I understood for the first time that I had lived my entire Christian life as a slave to sin. It was as though Jesus's words on the cross, "It is finished" (John 19:30), applied to others but not to me.

Scripture awakened for me with freshness and clarity. I could read it through a new lens—the lens of grace—and it began to set my heart free. Jesus spoke these words in John 8:32: "Then you will know the truth, and the truth will set you free." Truth can't be logic in your head alone. It needs to bring liberation to your daily life. Little by little, the prison doors of my heart began to come loose of their chains.

Unlocking the Pain

During the second year of my healing journey, my younger sister called me to tell me she remembered being sexually abused by my father. She was not alone in that experience. He also sexually violated me. A lot. Until I was in a safe environment, the trauma was too terrifying and shame producing for me to face. Acknowledging this painful piece of my history was overwhelming yet necessary. It unlocked the secret of the pain that fueled my rage. It was a giant step on the pathway to recovery from the shame of my childhood.

Up until this time, God remained a distant figure in my mind. His power, character, and love were truths I grasped in my head but not my heart. I knew of God, knew He was almighty, but my shame told me His power and love were for others and not for me. Jesus's death on the cross for my sin meant little to me. It didn't make me weep. I knew nothing of its worth except in theory. I lived a joyless and meaningless Christian life even though I longed for something else. Skepticism emerged in my thoughts. *Jesus died on the cross. Big deal. What does that have to do with the hell I am experiencing? I don't feel His love. I can't stop raging. I have a mountain of pain and brokenness that is my life, and I have no idea how to be free from it.* The words sounded like my prayer from ten years before when I told God there must be something supernatural involved with my sin in order for me to heal. He remembered that prayer and was in the process of answering it. I just didn't know it.

Chapter 2

IDEAL SELF, SHAME SELF, AND REAL SELF

As I began healing, I experienced a growing awareness of my shame. Shame was one of those words I could use in an academic way, understanding its meaning, but not fully grasping it. Shame meant feeling guilty and the embarrassment of being wrong. That was the best I knew of it in the beginning.

Growing up, I often read the story in Genesis when Adam and Eve were in the garden of Eden. They sinned, and they felt shame. I comprehended that. As a result of their sin, they recognized their nakedness, covered themselves with fig leaves, and hid in the trees. It wasn't wrong they were naked. The sin they committed exposed them, and nakedness exemplified their knowledge. I related to the feeling of guilt, shame, and the ensuing desire to hide after sin, but that was about where it ended for me.

Along with everything else I was being taught in my new church, I began a long journey to understand this experience of shame. I learned that guilt and shame were not the same experience. Guilt occurs when I have *done something wrong*. Shame is my self-assessment when I believe there *is something wrong* with me. I soon discovered I had lived my whole life feeling shame.

Carrying Shame

I felt shame when my father did and said socially unacceptable things in public. I felt shame when I said my last name, not wanting to be associated with my parents. I felt shame when I walked into school each day wearing unstylish clothes or shoes. I felt shame when I wasn't allowed to shave my legs. I felt shame when I couldn't wear makeup and perceived I was unattractive. I felt shame when my parents told me my personality was wrong. They said godly women were quiet and unobtrusive. I was loud, stubborn, and liked to be in charge. They told me I was too active in utero and kicked my mother more than I should have. I was given the message in countless ways that the core of my being was wrong. There was something inherently flawed in me, and therefore I shouldn't be cherished.

In addition, I carried the shame of the sexual abuse. Shame within me ran deep. My father had no conscience for his actions, so the shame transferred to me. I carried it for him. He was the head of the home. He was the one who twisted Scripture to give him authority for his actions. The ugliness of his sin seeped under my skin and took root in my soul. I believed I was raw sewage.

Oh, that I could hide behind a tree like Adam and Eve and not be seen. I was certain everyone could see it on my face. They could see the ugliness. They could see the filth that was me. I longed to be cherished and wanted. My father told me he loved me. It was a lie. His actions did not display love. Only someone who is despised and worthless is treated like this. I felt used and tossed aside like a dirty rag. I didn't feel beautiful. I felt repulsive. I wore ugly clothes, had an ugly face, and wore the ugliness of my father's sin against me in my very being. I was shame itself.

My Fig Leaves

Shame bears the lie that we will not be loved or valued if it is seen. Like Adam and Eve, we need to find a way to hide it. I created many sophisticated fig leaves to hide my shame, leaves birthed in my childhood. Since I carried the shame from my childhood into my adult life, I carried the fig leaves with me as well. I believed I wouldn't be respected without them.

We attempt to hide shame in multiple ways, but one fig leaf I used often was perfectionism. I reasoned that if I am perfect, I am safe. If I never made a mistake, my father had no reason to abuse me, and no one would recognize my unworthiness. I was driven to be perfect. I required perfect grades, perfect obedience to my parents, and a perfect performance as a Christian. As I dragged this self-protective pattern into my adult life, I needed to have a perfectly clean home, a stainless performance at my job, and well-behaved children so I would be regarded as a successful mother. As all perfectionists know, achieving anything less than 100 percent in your performance is unacceptable. Hitting below that mark means failure. As soon as a mistake happens, the curtain rises, and the truth is revealed on stage for all to see.

Perfectionism never lasts as a successful covering of our shame. Just like the fig leaves didn't work for Adam and Eve, this fig leaf struck out for me. Robert S. McGee, in his book *The Complete Search for Significance*, said it well: "Shame often engulfs us when a flaw in our performance is so important, so overpowering, or so disappointing to us that it creates a permanently negative opinion about our self-worth. Others may not know of our failure, but we do. We may only imagine their rejection, but real or imagined, the pain resulting from it cripples our confidence and hope."[1]

Another sophisticated fig leaf I used was my need to feel superior. It was my roundabout way of trying to feel better about myself. If I was perfect, I believed I was righteous enough to be the source of judgment on the rest of the world. Since I didn't do what others did and did what others should have done, I could feel superior. In so doing, arrogance kept me from the stink of my shame. I was aware of the harm of my criticism but needed to keep it up to gain some measure of self-respect. There had to be a way I wasn't always the least wanted person. When I walked into a room of people, I sized everyone up, hoping there might be someone who had something undesirable about them I might feel superior to. Without it, in my mind, I had nothing.

Then I held the fig leaf of my anger. My rage. The power within me I couldn't control. I hated it and I loved it. I hated it because I couldn't shrink from the reality that rage is listed in Scripture as an expression of our flesh. Anger is an emotion, which is not wrong. Even God feels anger. But rage is anger out of control. My rage demonstrated I was a dirty, rotten sinner. No amount of teaching Sunday school or not cheating on a test in college would be enough to erase the sinfulness in me that my rage exposed. On the other hand, I loved my rage because it made me feel powerful. I hated the impotence of being a victim at my father's hand or by anyone I perceived took advantage of me. When I raged, I felt strong. I felt in control, even though I was completely out of control. It was a way of deflecting the shame I felt. When I raged, my shame didn't define me. I was a strong woman who could stand for herself and demand justice.

Another fig leaf came in the form of desserts. *Ah, desserts.* When someone hurt me and confirmed my belief I would never be loved, I could find solace in a bowl of ice cream, a handful of cookies, or a piece of cake. In each bite, the pleasure of the sweet treat seemed to melt away the emotional pain for a moment. It offered a break from the anguish because no one could take the pleasure of the delicious bite away. I experienced what I wanted when I wanted it. No matter that it left me pudgy and full of shame for my pudginess, because for those few minutes, I had relief.

I used other fig leaves less often, but they came in handy when needed. The fig leaf of blame allowed me to blame others when my mistakes and character defects were brought to light. The fig leaf of hiding (physically) and isolating (emotionally) made me believe others wouldn't walk away from me. They couldn't walk away from what they didn't know. Sometimes my fig leaf was denial, usually through revisionist history, to change the story even a little bit so I didn't look so bad. My fig leaf of people pleasing looked like kindness when it was, in truth, self-serving. I gave others what they wanted, making my voice and desires disappear, so they wanted to be with me. Adam and Eve's fig leaves were temporary fixes, just like these fig leaves were for me.

Perceived Control

None of the effects of my parents' abuse faded when I moved across the country. I carried the shame and my self-protective fig leaves with me wherever I went. The fig leaves showed up at college and in my marriage, friendships, work environments, and parenting. I responded to people with the rage that should have been reserved for my parents. *Why did I overreact in rage like that?*

I was convinced that I was worthless. I had plenty of evidence to prove that fact. Even though I tried to feel better about myself through arrogant superiority, I knew I didn't have what it took to be a "good Christian." I was certain I would never be treated with dignity and value but didn't want anyone to know it. If anything happened to expose my humanity, my sin, or my weakness, I deflected it in some way with one of my fig leaves.

I desperately needed to control how I was perceived. I wanted to be my *ideal self*, the one to be admired and respected instead of disregarded. I didn't want to be my *real self*, the person who was flawed and unacceptable.

My ideal self was thin and stylish, kind and gracious, patient and even-tempered, successful, respected at work, with a beautiful and perpetually tidy home, an adoring husband, and well-behaved happy children. I believed if I were that person, I would be valued. I would be accepted. I would be respected. I would be loved.

Since I was not the ideal person I wanted to be, I was what I believed in my shame. I was my *shame self*. My shame self was ugly, overweight, frumpy, easily provoked to anger, undisciplined, behind in my work, a critical wife, and a clueless mother. I despised these self-perceptions and wanted to be viewed as my ideal self. I felt the need to control my circumstances so others saw only what I wanted them to see. I couldn't let people discover my untidy house with our hand-me-down furniture that didn't match. In response to this fear, I didn't invite anyone into our home and flew into a cleaning frenzy if anyone stopped by unannounced. I couldn't let anyone see that I didn't know what I was doing as a parent, so I mimicked what I saw other parents do, acting like I knew all along. No one could know I watched television because some in my friend circles considered it lazy, unintelligent, or unspiritual.

God forbid I would ever say aloud that I raged at my husband and children for the ways I believed they unveiled my shame. Because I saw my husband and children as an extension of myself, anything they did or said that showed their humanness divulged my defectiveness. Their mistakes and imperfections were my mistakes and imperfections. I didn't want my weaknesses bared, nor did I want their weaknesses exposed. I tried to control what they said and did so my ideal self was perceived. If they were flawless, then I was a success. If this were true, I would be loved, admired, and respected. The amount of hurt and damage I created for my husband and children through this control is immeasurable.

Criticism's Reflection

In my arrogant superiority, I felt I had the right to judge others by incriminating their motives and deciding their sins. In my mind, this pretense gave me the right to tell them what to do. I often believed the lie that in sharing with others what they *should* do and say, I helped them. "Just do what I tell you to do, and your life will be better," I determined. I had no idea that this judgmental criticism reflected my shame, revealing it as the driving force of my life. Only a shame-filled person would be shameless in their lack of compassion toward others' humanity. And that shame-filled person was me.

I criticized my parents because they were judgmental and prideful, yet I was also haughty. Though my actions were different than my parents' abuse, my behaviors were destructive and hurtful toward those I influenced. Without healing and learning a new way, it was inevitable I would behave and sin in some of the ways my parents did. God knew—and held His hope for me when I had none. He knew how to help me when I didn't know how to help myself. He took me step by step down the healing path.

Chapter 3
Sin's Gaping Wound

Rick saw through what I tried to hide. He discerned my struggle with shame and the harmful self-protection I used attempting to cover it. He observed the control, arrogance, rage, and perfectionism, then, in his wisdom, slowly held up a mirror to me.

In one of our meetings, as we talked about the destruction from my parents, I spewed to Rick, "I would *never* molest a child!"

He was quiet, then responded with insight. "Guess what, Louise? You don't get brownie points for not doing a sin you're not tempted to do. What are you going to do about your judgmental, critical heart?"

His words of loving rebuke were used by God to enlighten me. They began to humble and free me. His correction showed me I wasn't pleasing to God for what I did or didn't do. My striving didn't make me better in God's sight. Just because my sins were more socially acceptable than my parents' sins, I remained guilty before God. I believed I was above doing anything my parents had done. My sins weren't as bad as theirs. In my pride, I thought myself superior to them, giving me the right to judge them.

All sin stinks, and all sin is destructive. My sin of judgmental criticism revealed my lack of personal righteousness. Owning it knocked me off my self-created pedestal and into a rightful place of being imperfect like everyone else. Recognizing my self-righteous sin showed me I needed Jesus's work on the cross after I became a Christian as much as I needed His work for my salvation. Hearing this truth helped me begin to face my sins. It was a critical step in the journey of slow release from the performance trap that had held me in bondage for thirty years.

Healthy Shame

In the moment of my pastor's loving correction, I was, perhaps for the very first time, experiencing healthy shame. Healthy shame says, "I have awareness that I am not God. I am imperfect. I sin. I make mistakes. I have done something wrong. I humbly acknowledge my need for God and others. I cannot do life alone." The only other time I had experienced anything like this was when I was a little girl on the hill in front of my house and asked Jesus to be my Savior. My childlike faith came out of my need for Jesus, and He responded to me. Because of the theology of my childhood, I tried to please God by my efforts. Living by this self-improvement plan exhausted me. It hurt me and others. And it didn't work. Healthy shame would have brought me to Jesus in humble trust and dependency. I had no understanding of this helpful state before God and others until I looked honestly at my sin and the motive behind it.

The parable of the Pharisee and the tax collector in Luke 18 provides a powerful illustration of healthy shame. The Pharisee, like me, was full of arrogant superiority and lacked awareness of his need for a Savior. In contrast, the tax collector found freedom in owning his brokenness and asking for help. He cried, "God, have mercy on me, a sinner." Humility creates a breakthrough and willingness to depend on someone other than yourself.

Healthy shame allows me to be my *real self*. Healthy shame balances the significance of my dignity and the truth of my ability to act selfishly. Healthy shame says I have value and at the same time admits I am human. Living this way creates safety to be honest about personal strengths and weaknesses. It opens the door for a life of openhearted interdependency. Psychologist John Bradshaw, in his best-selling book *Healing the Shame that Binds You*, described healthy shame in this way: "It is necessary to feel shame if one is to be truly human. Shame is the emotion that gives us permission to be human. Shame tells us of our limits. Shame keeps us in our human boundaries, letting us know we can and will make mistakes and that we need help. Our shame tells us we are not God. Healthy shame is the psychological foundation of humility. It is the source of spirituality."[2]

Destructive Shame

All I had known of shame up to this point was unhealthy shame—the destructive shame that is a part of our flesh, the place where sin resides in us. Destructive shame is a tool of the Evil One to accuse and rob us of joy, peace, and hope. Destructive shame says, "I am worthless. I will never measure up. I don't have what it takes. I am unlovable. I will never experience love, acceptance, belonging, and fulfillment. I will never be valued, and I will be alone. There is something inherently wrong with me." Shame is often described as an emotion, but it can also be a state of being or thinking, a way of seeing everything and everyone.

Note: In this book, when we speak of destructive shame, we will call it "shame." When we refer to *healthy* shame, we will name it as such.

When I am harmed as a human being and that hurt remains unaddressed, a shame veil comes over my eyes and I no longer see clearly. My view is distorted. As additional harm is done, more veils cover my eyes so I become blinded to the truth of what I see and experience. The more shame I carry, the more this distortion causes me to react to my relationships and circumstances in an out-of-balance way.

In destructive shame, every slight I perceive, every rejection I feel, every mistake I make, every contest I lose, every sin I repeat, and every relationship that fails only adds to the pile of evidence I have accumulated, proving what I believe about my worth. The bigger the pile of evidence, the more shame has a hold on me. The way I saw it, the pile that proved my worthlessness was ten feet tall. Not only was my shame evidence heaped with the message of my childhood abuse, but the pile also contained the times someone ridiculed me for my hairy legs, my lack of makeup, or my unstylish clothes. As I got older, the evidence stacked up with boyfriends who lost interest in me, a body type that looked more matronly than youthful, a big personality that intimidated people, and having no clue how to behave like a normal human being. In addition, I felt shame for my rage, arrogance, extra pounds, and judgmental heart.

A Gaping Wound

Every experience in my pile of evidence represented an unaddressed hurt I bore, whether it was something I did or that was done to me. As the evidence of my deficiencies stacked up, so grew my desire to hide. My fear of being exposed revealed itself by an advancing intensity of overreacting.

It was as if I had a gaping wound on my arm that never healed—an infection that made me sick. I was sensitive to it, protecting it intensely. If touched, the unhealed wound would bring me great pain, as though time had passed with no change since the original injury occurred. Because the first cut never healed, the wound became intolerable. If anyone so much as brushed past it, I might scream out in pain.

This wound that manifested in me was not a physical wound. It was an emotional, relational, and spiritual wound caused by my parents' abuse. Without healing the original relational wound, the wound turned into shame. The shame wound then became infected and filled with pus. It oozed and smelled, and everyone around could see it, even when I did my best to cover it with skillfully crafted fig leaves.

Overreacting

When my husband and I were first married and he did anything I interpreted as taking advantage of me, like not picking up his dirty laundry off the floor, I reacted in shame. I didn't respectfully say, "You're a grown man. I trust you to pick up your underwear yourself." Instead I railed at him, calling him a selfish jerk (or worse) at the top of my lungs, with the veins on my neck sticking out. I was not responding to his need to mature as an adult. I viewed his behavior and the motive of his behavior through the thick veils of my shame. When he brushed by my old shame wound by not picking up his underwear, it told me, "You are not worthy to be cherished. You are only to be used." I was 3 percent responding to his youthful wish that I would be like his mother and pick up his underwear for him and 97 percent reacting to the pain of the years of abuse at my father's hand.

My overreactions displayed what William Cloke noted in his article "Rage, Shame, and the Death of Love": "Rage is aroused by an event that mirrors a primary emotional injury."[3] My responses to slight offenses were overreactions. I wasn't only reacting to the slight. I was reacting to the original wound that remained unhealed.

Overreaction to ordinary life experiences reveals that something happened to us long ago that is not yet healed. If one is told as a child that they will never amount to anything, these words cut the child to the heart. If this emotional and spiritual wound remains unhealed, the child will carry these words and wounds throughout their life, into their adulthood, fearing them to be true. When anyone does or says anything that in their mind confirms what they were told, they will respond in one of two ways: They will pour poisonous condemning words back on themselves in self-contempt, heaping more shame upon the open wound and infecting it more. Or they will spew poisonous, condemning words on the person who has intentionally or unintentionally brushed past their unhealed wound, trying in vain to bring air to the wound in order to heal it, but instead infecting the wound once again.

Covering My Face

Dear friends from my home group at church, Kenny and Judi, visited their daughter who taught English in South Korea. When they returned, they shared with our group about their trip. They told of the delicious food, the masses of people that squeezed onto the subway train during rush hour, and of the only beggar they saw on the streets. He begged while lying with his face to the ground. This precious man, close to God's heart, demonstrated the ultimate picture of destructive shame. In his neediness, he begged, but as he did he protected himself from being seen and protected the passersby from having to look upon his shame. The poor have much to teach us.

We are not so different from this beggar. I don't want you to see my shame, because if you do, I believe you won't value me or desire a relationship with me. Because of that, I will do whatever it takes to hide the pile of evidence for my shame from you. Psalm 44:15 says, "My disgrace is before me all day long, and my face is covered with shame."

In Michael Lewis's scholarly book on shame, *Shame, the Exposed Self*, he wrote about Charles Darwin's study of shame: "The opinions of others about our appearance, especially the appearance of our faces, or our conduct, are Darwin's elicitors of shame. . . . He was clear in specifying that action per se is not the cause of the shame state: shame arises from how others see us. Understand here that the metaphorical 'see' means 'evaluate.'"⁴ Because I know that I see and evaluate others, I assume they see and evaluate me. Since I could see through others' fig leaves, I feared they could see through mine to the shame self I attempted to hide.

The Relational Experience

Shame is a relational experience. We are beings designed by God for connection (Gen. 2:18), and thus we long for a place to belong—a place to be valued and loved. We cannot experience giving and receiving love and respect unless we are with others. Shame hinders us from stepping into relationships where love is expressed freely. If I believe I am my shame self, I will live alone, even if I am surrounded by people, because I will hide, fearing rejection. I know this because I did it. In my younger years, I knew others, but they didn't fully know me. I hid what I believed were the unpresentable parts of me, all in effort to display my ideal self so I might be accepted.

When I am in a mindset of destructive shame, I believe a lie. In that state, I have proof that my assessment is correct. The pile of evidence for my insignificance showed there was something ugly and distasteful about me, something worthless and disgusting, and that is why I was used and tossed aside as a child. I noticed how others were cherished, protected, and wanted. In my view, something was beautiful and delightful about them that I didn't possess. I judged myself as unworthy of love and respect because of experiences that I believed defined me. I've learned that though I fear the judgment and criticism of others, most often the chief judge and critic of me is *me*. Now I look back and wonder how many times I believed someone judged or criticized me when they didn't.

I want to be loved and valued. I want to experience the respect of others. I want to have self-respect. Sin robs me of respect because sin brings destruction. It destroys and kills. When you sin against me, you put a dent in my dignity, and when I sin against you, I do the same to you. If a video showed me acting foolish and destructive by eating a whole sleeve of Girl Scouts Thin Mints (not that I have *ever* done this), you would see me disrespecting myself. If you witnessed someone screaming obscenities at me, you would see in my face the harm of the slander. If you saw me criticizing someone, the sin would wound the spirit of both me and the one I offended. The sin creates the shame. The sin mars our dignity.

When sin does its virulent work, it creates a feeling of nakedness and exposure. Sin harms. Nothing within us is able to recover on our own from sin's destruction. We were not created with the ability to absorb the effects of it in us. We need something greater than ourselves to deal with it. We need Jesus. The more we understand about shame, the clearer this reality becomes.

Chapter 4

SELF-PROTECTION'S ILLUSION

When I was ten years old, my family went on our annual visit to our grandparents' homes in Chicago and Milwaukee. Our Chevrolet Corvair, after many years of use, was beyond repair, and my parents didn't have funds to replace it. I went with my dad to visit my paternal grandfather in his apartment after the car broke down. My dad mentioned to his father what happened with the car. My grandfather opened his wallet and pulled out ten one-hundred-dollar bills, an eye-popping experience for me, and handed them to my father, instructing him to get what he needed. My father told his dad he would pay him back. At that moment, my violent, alcoholic grandfather generously came through for my dad, and we went to purchase a used Oldsmobile Cutlass. (Those were the days when $1,000 could buy a good used car.)

Years later, I asked my father if he ever paid his dad back the money advanced to him.

"No," my father responded. "He owes me."

Of course, my father never loaned my grandfather a nickel. We were the ones struggling to pay bills and put food on the table. What my father felt his dad owed him was not money but payback for the hurt and pain the turbulent physical abuse of his childhood created.

Debt Collection

For decades I had the same posture toward my parents. In my judgment, they owed me for what was done to me. They needed to suffer in the same way I suffered from their ill-treatment of me. I fantasized that I'd get even. They would pay for what they did. In my dreams I found myself screaming at my parents for their abuse. They took something from me that needed to be restored. The debt they owed was not just about the money to cover the professional counseling I needed.

> A pastor, counselor, or anyone who works closely with human beings knows this whole debt system has been built into the human personality in a most incredible fashion. There is a sense of *oughtness*, of *owing* a debt, an automatic mechanism by which the built-in debt collectors go to work. We seek to atone for those wrongs, to pay the debt we owe, or to collect the debt that someone else owes us. If we feel anger at ourselves, we say, "I must pay in full." Or if we feel anger at someone else, he or she must pay. In this way the whole inexorable process is set in motion as the personality is turned over to the inner tormentors. They are the jailers who work as the debt collectors in this awful prison.[5]
> —David A. Seamands, *Healing for Damaged Emotions*

Sin's Consequences

Our sin has both relational and spiritual consequences. We hurt people. We hurt ourselves. We hurt God. All sin is *relational*. Even the sin we do in secret brings destruction to us and to those we love—and hurts the heart of God. We may not see the harm we create immediately, but it will catch up to us. Often others can recognize our destructive and hurtful behaviors and the effects of them before we become willing to admit it.

All sin is *spiritual*. I take something intangible from you when I sin against you. Just ask someone who has been hurt by my selfishness. A spiritual and relational debt is created when sin occurs. When I sin against you, you have a sense that I owe you something, even when I have not taken your money. When you sin against me, I think, *You owe me*. Why would I think this unless something relational and spiritual has been taken from me? My dignity has been taken. Respect has been stolen from me. I mistakenly believe that if my offender somehow pays me back, the dent in my dignity will be restored. *Give me back what you have taken*.

Futile Attempts

A spiritual problem needs a spiritual solution. A relational problem needs a relational solution. Shame is both a spiritual problem and a relational problem. Only God can offer the spiritual and relational solutions needed for the problem of shame. Only Jesus can restore our dignity. Author Bill Tell, in his book *Lay It Down*, said, "Therefore, as Adam and Eve discovered and as we learn in our futile attempts to cure our shame, our shame necessitates a redemptive solution. It requires the gospel."[6]

My attempts to cover the shame that came from my parents' sin against me not only didn't work to cover my shame but also brought me more destruction. These self-protective strategies—my fig leaves—were rooted in a belief that I had to take care of myself. I didn't trust others to meet my relational needs. I certainly didn't trust God to take care of me. Look what He allowed to happen. God wanted me to learn to depend on Him, to trust Him with my heart, and I would have none of it. I liked my sophisticated fig leaves and the sense of safety they gave me. I enjoyed the illusion of control and the counterfeit experience of my relational needs being met.

I was resistant to think of my self-protective strategies as being sinful. My motive seemed innocent. I was trying to keep myself from being hurt. Who would blame me after all I had been through? Yes, I needed to give myself grace for not knowing another way to survive as a child. I didn't need to beat myself up for that. But I was no longer a child and needed to mature into a healthier style of relational interaction—and I didn't want to. In truth, I was physiologically an adult but emotionally still a child. I didn't recognize that my self-protection affected others. I saw no harm in my behaviors because my strategies made me feel safe. I didn't understand that when I kept an imaginary wall around my heart, I was not just trying to keep myself from being hurt, I was, in the process, hurting others.

Self-Protection

I obtained a bachelor of arts degree in vocal performance. As a skilled classical musician, I sang German lieder and opera arias for my recitals. I was a trusted soloist for Handel's "Messiah" at Christmastime. In the era of church worship music led through choirs, organs, and pianos, I fit right in. I loved to sing. When we started attending our new church in 1989, their worship was led by singers with electric guitars and drums. I sang on occasion but feared I would be mocked for my trained voice.

As God began to free me in my healing journey, I was once again asked to sing a solo during a Sunday morning service. A good friend came to me afterward and said, "I enjoyed your singing today, Louise. It was better. You were humble this time."

My friend's words might as well have stuck a knife right into my heart. I was stymied as to how to respond. I felt insecure when I sang in the past at our church. Why would she say what she did? I had not felt superior to anyone when I sang, fearing their rejection.

As I pondered my friend's words, I realized what she meant. In my fear, I put a three-foot-thick imaginary wall around my heart to protect myself from others' negative evaluations. My friend didn't see that wall as an effort to guard myself. She saw that wall as my pride, and when I was boldly honest with myself, I knew it to be true. I was proud. I didn't want to let God or any of my dear friends in. I wasn't humble in the true sense of the word. I trusted only myself.

When I self-protect, it is hard to face the harm of the imaginary wall because I feel afraid and small without it. However, in doing so, I cover my shame with sin. It is like using the E. coli bacteria to heal a kidney infection. Sin cannot and will not heal shame. If I don't trust and don't think I have anywhere else to turn, I will use counterfeits of true trust and love to protect myself because they trick me into believing I am doing something good about my shame. Those counterfeits are an illusion—and they are sin.

When I carry shame, I don't believe anyone will have my back. I must therefore protect myself in whatever way will assuage the angst, even for a few moments. When I sang and had the wall up around my heart, I felt safe, but I came across as proud to my friend. I didn't trust the listeners with my voice. I didn't believe God would defend me if I were mocked for my singing. In my pride and unbelief, I trusted only me to take care of me.

Trusting Myself

Our flesh, the seat of sin in us, wants to live independent of God. I want to be in charge. I want to be like God. I don't want to risk trusting and believing Him, so, like Adam and Eve, I find fig leaves and a tree, attempting to care for myself and cover my shame. The coverings I create for myself are sin. Each fig leaf is me putting my fist in the air to God to say that I will not trust Him. I will not depend on Him. I will do it myself. I will create my own god to take care of me.

Today, few would create a statue made of wood or stone and pray to it, but we regularly fashion more palatable (to us) idols rather than making ourselves vulnerable to God. Romans 1:25 says, "They exchanged the truth of God for a lie, and worshiped and served created things rather than the Creator—who is forever praised. Amen." When we make our own covering for our shame, we turn from our true protector to what we believe protects us. We turn to ourselves.

> It is man's fuel for burning;
>> some of it he takes and warms himself,
>> he kindles a fire and bakes bread.
> But he also fashions a god and worships it;
>> he makes an idol and bows down to it.
> Half of the wood he burns in the fire;
>> over it he prepares his meal,
>> he roasts his meat and eats his fill.
> He also warms himself and says,
>> "Ah! I am warm; I see the fire."
> From the rest he makes a god, his idol;
>> he bows down to it and worships.
> He prays to it and says,
>> "Save me; you are my god."
> They know nothing, they understand nothing;
>> their eyes are plastered over so they cannot see,
>> and their minds closed so they cannot understand.
> No one stops to think,
>> no one has the knowledge or understanding to say,
> "Half of it I used for fuel;
>> I even baked bread over its coals,
>> I roasted meat and I ate.
> Shall I make a detestable thing from what is left?
>> Shall I bow down to a block of wood?"

He feeds on ashes, a deluded heart misleads him;
> he cannot save himself, or say,
> "Is not this thing in my right hand a lie?" (Isa. 44:15–20)

In the aftermath of my friend telling me, "You were humble this time," I realized the "thing in my right hand"—the wall I put around my heart—was a lie. It was an idol. It was my pride. It was my unbelief. It was sin. I trusted only myself. I did not trust God or anyone else with me. My wall did not heal or protect me. Instead, it harmed me and others.

God's Compassion

Every time I choose self-protection, I learn something. It reveals where I don't trust God with myself. It's understandable that all of us who have experienced abuse and neglect at the hands of those designed by God to love and protect us will have a hard time trusting. God knows this and offers great compassion to those harmed by grievous sin. Scripture is full of demonstrations and words of His compassion toward the oppressed. God cares about the pain and injustice we experience.

> The Lord is close to the brokenhearted
> > and saves those who are crushed in spirit. (Ps. 34:18)
> But you, O Lord, are a compassionate and gracious God,
> > slow to anger, abounding in love and faithfulness. (Ps. 86:15)
> The Lord works righteousness
> > and justice for all the oppressed. (Ps. 103:6)

God's empathy with our pain and fear to trust doesn't let us off the hook regarding looking at ourselves and naming what is true. Abused children need to find a way to survive, and there is great courage in that. When we become adults, there comes a time for us to face ourselves. This is true for all who have experienced relational hurt. When I protect myself, I say, "I can take care of me. I don't need you, God, and I don't need anyone else." In self-protecting, I was, in effect, refusing God's and others' protection of me. Since I didn't trust God or people, I wouldn't allow their care to reach me. The strategies of self-protection I used to survive as a child became destructive to me and others when I became an adult. I needed to admit that and learn to live another way. I needed to understand the nature of sin and the power of grace so I could learn God's healthy relational design.

Facing the Truth

Sin is anything that falls short of God's perfect righteousness. The Bible says, "All unrighteousness is sin" (1 John 5:17 KJV). Any behavior or thought that is not perfect by God's standards is a sin. Therein lies the rub. I can't be perfect. I can't be righteous. If I strive to be righteous in my own strength, it will be an exhausting effort, and I will never attain it. If I decide perfect righteousness and holiness is an unfair standard and thus decide *for myself* what is evil enough to be called a sin in order to minimize its destruction, I fool myself. Only a holy, perfect, and righteous God can declare what is unrighteous and imperfect. We, as imperfect people, cannot make this judgment. We are unqualified. Any moral decision that does not measure up to God's standard is sin.

As I began to face this truth, I did not like it one bit. I didn't believe it was fair. I should get to do whatever I need to do to protect myself because of what I experienced. My fear and pain were more important than whatever hurt others might experience as a result of my self-protection. I didn't want to learn to trust. How was I to trust God with my shame and my childhood relational and spiritual wounds when He allowed them? How was I ever to trust anyone when the ones closest to me had not been trustworthy?

Nancy, my selfless mentor who met with me for years, kept encouraging me to trust God instead of relying on myself. She knew what this trust would do to bring healing to my heart. In response to her prompts, I said to her, "But I don't trust God, Nancy. I do, however, trust hot fudge sundaes. When I am sad and feeling shame, hot fudge sundaes make me feel better for about three minutes. Until I trust God, I will go to hot fudge sundaes when I am sad." And so I did.

I didn't believe God would meet me in my pain in a way I liked. I wanted relief from the pain, and up to that point He didn't seem to be removing any of it. Numbing it seemed like a clever plan, but the problem was I became overweight and felt shame for those extra pounds because I was not my ideal self.

Here I was, eating hot fudge sundaes, cookies, or whatever numbed the pain for a little while. I raged to make myself feel powerful and was driven to perfectionism to maintain the image of my ideal self. I attempted to control the behaviors of my family members so they reflected me well. And I lived with a thick imaginary wall around my heart. I even had a name for the wall: the Great Wall of China.

These self-protective strategies gave me an illusion of safety. I wanted to keep everyone out of the deep places of my heart for fear I would be hurt again. If people got too close, they wouldn't like what they found in me. The problem was that behind the thick wall, behind those sophisticated fig leaves, I was alone, and I didn't experience love. Precious people came toward me to love me, and I never felt their love because it bounced off the wall. I didn't know how to let their love penetrate my heart. Even with those who deeply loved me, I couldn't recognize their love and didn't understand how to receive it. In his book *Lay It Down*, Bill Tell said, "Shame always leaves me unloved—no matter how much love others might have for me."[7]

Lack of Hope

Slowly I began to understand the feebleness of my strategies. The self-protective measures weren't helping me. Not only that, they didn't protect me. They harmed me and everyone around me. In attempting to cover my self-hatred, I dishonored those I loved by not giving them a chance to imperfectly love me. I wanted a guarantee that if I took down the imaginary wall around my heart even a tiny bit, I wouldn't be hurt. The self-protection did nothing to heal the shame and pain I carried. Psychologist Dan Allender, in his book *The Wounded Heart*, said, "The shame of folly is involved whenever our false god remains deaf and dumb, impotent to heal the wound of our heart."[8] The wall and my fig leaves were powerless to heal the wounds of my heart.

As silly as it sounds, the hot fudge sundaes were one of my idols. Other idols were my perfectionism, rage, controlling behaviors, denial, justifying, blaming, and people pleasing. Comprehending the futility of my self-protective schemes was a key step in my healing journey. My eyes were opened to how much I didn't trust God and others and how much I didn't want to. I was terrified to risk it.

As the reality came to light that the idols I trusted to protect me didn't protect me, I knew a change was needed. Like Adam and Eve in the garden, I understood I was naked. I knew I was not God and couldn't fix myself. I experienced healthy shame. I knew if I didn't learn trust and healthy dependency on God and others, I would never feel valued and loved. I had to take down my walls, come out from behind the trees, and throw away my fig leaves before I could heal. But where I was in my inability to trust God and others, I couldn't ever foresee that happening. However, God was not hindered by my lack of hope. He continued to make a way for me.

Chapter 5

THE SHAME-CONTEMPT DANCE

Shame and judgmental thoughts go hand in hand. You can't have one without the other. If one is deemed unworthy, it is because another has judged him to be so. This holds true whether the judge shames himself or another. When I speak *or think* shaming words about you, I condemn you. When I speak or think shaming words about myself, I condemn myself. This shaming judgment is contempt, which is disapproval tinged with disgust.

Contempt says, "You are worthless. You are despicable. How could you have done that? Don't you know better? Idiot." Foul language is an expression of contempt, as are curse words. A curse is a condemnation smeared in hatred. Contempt can take the form of disdain, mocking, bullying, hatred, scorn, malice, slander, prejudice, rage, accusation, neglect, fighting, or even war. It is the tongue of our flesh in its most sinister form.

The apostle Paul understood this and exhorted the believers in Colossae about it: "But now you must rid yourselves of all such things as these: anger, rage, malice, slander, and filthy language from your lips.

Do not lie to each other, since you have taken off your old self with its practices" (Col. 3:8–9).

Permission to Condemn

Christians in the United States have a widespread reputation for being judgmental and self-righteous. This must be grievous to God's heart. I have been guilty of this assessment. When I step into the role of judge toward myself or another, I give myself permission to devalue, condemn, or abuse. I step into this role of judge when I believe I am superior or more righteous than the one upon whom I pour contempt.

Without a true understanding of God's grace, I lived in performance mode—for both myself and others. Before my healing journey, the only theology I knew of grace was for salvation. I stood in judgment of those who were not, in my mind, as righteous as I was. My heart aches in memory of the contemptuous posture I have taken toward others. God, forgive me.

Unqualified to Judge

We are all broken in our humanity. We all need Jesus. Whether we struggle with socially acceptable or unacceptable sins, we fall short. Our pride and unbelief give us permission in our flesh, the seat of sin in us, to pronounce judgment on others. God, however, does not see it this way. Romans 2:1–3 tells us, "You, therefore, have no excuse, you who pass judgment on someone else, for at whatever point you judge the other, you are condemning yourself, because you who pass judgment do the same things. Now we know that God's judgment against those who do such things is based on truth. So when you, a mere man, pass judgment on them and yet do the same things, do you think you will escape God's judgment?"

When I believed I got brownie points for not doing a sin I wasn't tempted to do, I missed an important truth. My socially acceptable sins didn't make me superior to others. Everyone is guilty before God. When, in humility, I grasp this truth, I understand that I am wholly unqualified to judge anyone. Dan Allender, in his pioneering book on sexual abuse, *The Wounded Heart*, said it with straightforward boldness: "Genuine conviction of sin . . . leads to a softening of the heart that dispels other-centered contempt in the wake of the recognition that we are no better, at core, than those who have abused us."[9]

Oftentimes my sin of contempt shows up while I am driving. If I'm driving on the freeway and someone swerves past me, almost hitting me at seventy-five miles an hour, I'm startled. A few seconds later, it dawns on me that a dangerous accident could have happened. Then it hits me. I have been disrespected. The reckless driver put everyone on the freeway in harm's way. Only God knows the full motive of their unsafe driving. Perhaps they were speeding to a hospital with someone having a heart attack or a woman in labor. I rarely think of those possibilities. Instead, I assume they are selfishly disrespecting everyone on the freeway. When I think this, I become their judge and start spouting shaming and contemptuous words aloud or in my thoughts. I say, "Idiot. Who do they think they are to drive like that? They could have killed someone."

In shame and contempt, we assume motive. Convinced our interpretation of the actions or words of the one who disrespects or hurts us is correct, we judge their motive as selfish. "They meant to disregard me. They only care about themselves. They don't think about how they affect me." Sometimes people are selfish and hurt with intention, but when we view our lives through veils of shame, we judge others with contempt because of our assumption of their motive.

Our Dance

Shame, contempt, judgment, and criticism can appear anywhere and with anyone we meet, but they show up strongest in our closest relationships. In intimate connections these shame-based responses can cause great damage. I can't count how many thousands of times I have accused and hurt my dear husband in this way. Though he is human and can at times be selfish, in truth, he is one of the kindest, gentlest human beings on the planet and wants to love me well.

For the first twelve years of our marriage—almost every day—Chuck and I acted out what I call the shame-contempt dance. Our skill at this destructive dance harmed us and our children and robbed us of enjoying the good in each other. We danced this regularly:

1. I felt shame because of something he did or didn't do that touched the infected, open wound of my shame.

2. I reacted in contempt by criticizing him.

3. My words lanced the gaping unhealed wound of his shame.

4. He spoke words of contempt toward me.

5. His response confirmed what I believed about his lack of care for me, and his words brushed my shame wound once again.

6. I retaliated with more condemnation.

7. He responded in turn.

The shame and contempt fired back and forth, often escalating to verbal abuse on my part and his hardened heart toward me. Each time our hearts were beat up and bruised from the encounter without enough time to recover before our next dance began.

Misunderstanding My Husband

Outside of Chuck's love for God and his family, probably his greatest love in life is playing the pipe organ. He fell in love with the organ while in Catholic grade school. The nuns gave interested children an opportunity to play the chapel organ. It was the perfect instrument for Chuck as a combination of his masculinity and the seed of the musical intelligence he didn't know existed within him. He feels most fully alive when he plays the organ, and he plays it with gusto. He has three academic degrees in organ performance.

For many years I didn't understand Chuck's legitimate need for expression as a man and as a musician. I wrongly perceived his nightly routine of practicing the pipe organ at a local church. I saw his need through the veils of my shame. I believed he was out at night because he didn't want to be around me. In my contempt, I judged he wanted to have some fun and leave me with all the work of caring for the house and our children. My lack of understanding and support of his need, combined with my criticism of him, shamed him for being who he is.

Our shame-contempt dance played out like this:

Louise: "You're late. You said that you would be home at eight o'clock, and it is eight thirty."

Chuck: "I know. I was working on the Buxtehude, and then Mark came by. We started talking, and I lost track of time."

Louise: "Why didn't you call? You could have called, and you didn't."

Chuck: "You knew where I was. You knew I'd get home when I was done. Why are you making such a big deal of all of this?"

Louise: "Don't you think I have stuff to do too? I have to prepare my lesson for school tomorrow and cut out a hundred stars for a learning center for my preschool students. If you're off playing the organ, having fun, and I'm sitting here taking care of the kids the whole night, when am I supposed to get that done?"

Chuck: "Can't you do it now? The kids are in bed, and you could work on it and probably have it done soon."

Louise: "That's not the point. You get to go have fun and be like an irresponsible teenager with no responsibilities while I stay home and take care of everything."

Chuck: "There you go again. Why do you have to disrespect my organ playing? I have to do this, Louise. It is who I am. You're so demanding and critical."

Louise: "And why do you always take advantage of me? Why do I always have to do all of the work around here?"

Chuck: "Are you saying I never do anything for our family? What about the car? I took the car to get an oil change. I—"

Louise: "Big freakin' deal! One oil change? I do absolutely everything else! When are you going to grow up? When am I going to be a priority to you? I know you don't want to be around me."

Chuck: "As a matter of fact, who would want to be around you when you yell and criticize all the time?"

Louise: "You're a jerk. A selfish jerk."

Chuck: "How dare you? How dare you talk to me like that? I'm your husband!"

Louise: "And how dare you treat me like you do? I'm your wife! You treat me like dirt. You act like I am your hired hand to do everything around here. I hate my life!"

When I perform a dance like this with Chuck or anyone else, I believe my hurt is greater than the other person's hurt. Therefore I should get to say whatever I want whenever I want. My needs trump theirs. God is not going to meet my needs and care for me, so I must defend myself.

Toxic Communication

Shame and the brokenness it creates can destroy relationships. When two people repeatedly perform the shame-contempt dance, it is difficult for trust to develop or for healthy intimacy to grow. Both people put their walls up. The other is often perceived as the enemy, even as family members. In this dance, each partner is focused on protecting himself or herself, therefore making it a clumsy encounter, stepping on each other's toes.

Which dancer hurts the most? Who has done the most harm? Both are injured. Whenever we play the part of the judge, deciding who is *more* right and who is *more* wrong, we miss the point of the conflict. Believing that winning an argument is a victory is to lose the argument altogether. The effect of this kind of communication style on a relationship is toxic.

What Chuck and I did in trying to stand up for ourselves and demand not to be shamed was to shame each other. Michael Lewis spoke of this in his book *Shame, the Exposed Self* as he described an interaction between a husband and wife: "Unbeknownst to the husband, his 'suggestions' are shaming for his wife. He thinks he is only making suggestions. She reads his 'suggestions' as criticism, and feels shame. She responds to her sense of shame with withdrawal, depression, and anger. He reads her withdrawal as the withdrawal of love, and he, in turn, is shamed by it. They, like many couples, have created a shame environment in which each shames the other."[10]

I didn't understand this relational dynamic for years. For me, like football coach Vince Lombardi, winning was the only thing.[11] I held my ground and often refused to hear Chuck's side in our arguments. I believed whatever stand he took held no validity. At least it was not nearly as important as my view. In doing so, I poured contempt on him, adding credence, in his mind, to the lie of his shame that there was something wrong with him because he was a musician.

All Chuck could see in me was my self-righteous judgment. He couldn't see the pain in my heart. He didn't understand the shame wounds from my childhood. All he experienced were the effects of my brokenness on him. I couldn't see his pain or shame either because

I focused on myself. What I wanted from him was compassion and nurturing for the wounds of the abuse on my feminine soul. Because I was like a porcupine 98 percent of the time, and a porcupine that shot out poisonous quills at that, it was challenging for him to come near me. This, in turn, triggered my shame, which fueled my contemptuous thoughts toward him—and the dance continued.

What a shame-based environment we created for our children. How were they to grow up to be strong, confident women when their parents were not strong or confident? God knew and brought about the healing needed so we could, in time, model a different relational style for them. Step by step He changed and grew us, teaching us to live in a new way.

Chapter 6

PERFORMANCE TO GRACE

After two years of meeting every other week with Rick, we sat one Friday afternoon chipping away at the mountain of issues I carried into my adult life. While I don't recall the rest of our conversation, I do remember his question for me.

"Louise, why do you think I meet with you?"

I pondered for a moment, then began to cry. All I could do in response to his question was weep. In wisdom he waited for me. My tears seemed to rise from the deepest part of my soul. I struggled to find the words to answer him. After what seemed like a good thirty minutes, I sputtered out my answer.

"You meet with me . . . because . . . you love me."

Crack. A hairline fracture split the wall around my heart. I risked opening my heart to Rick. He had earned my trust and helped me speak the truth aloud for my sake. His slow and painstaking work demonstrated he was different than every other male in authority I had ever experienced. He knew how hard this journey would be and established that it was possible for me to trust someone. He knew if I could trust one person, a foundational step in my healing from shame would occur. If I could trust him with me, I could risk trusting others who proved themselves trustworthy. When the wall of my heart cracked open, the love my pastor had shown me all along penetrated my heart because I let it, and in so doing, I felt his love.

Before that day, I had limited experience with being loved. Although I longed to be accepted and valued, I didn't understand that I would never experience love until I learned to trust. I would never feel acceptance until I allowed myself to be known. I would never feel valued until I stopped performing and lived as my real self. When I live without a wall, without pretending to be what my fig leaves portray me to be, my real self can be embraced and respected. Brennan Manning said in *A Glimpse of Jesus: Stranger to Self-Hatred*, "Self-hatred stands as an insuperable obstacle to growth and maturity. It derails interaction with others and renders us impotent to give or receive love."[12] My wall and fig leaves prevented me from experiencing love.

Environments of Grace

My newborn trust in Rick paved the way for me to begin to trust others. For me to continue to grow, I needed safe opportunities to practice authenticity with trustworthy people besides him. This brought up several questions. How would I find friends who would accept and value me as he did? Was my pastor a unique case? What frees people to offer this kind of love and acceptance? How would I discern someone's trustworthiness? Rick was a good man, but he wasn't perfect. Flawlessness couldn't be the measure. What makes a person safe?

I learned that relational safety is birthed in grace. God's grace. When grace is the foundation of a relationship or organization, it changes the dynamic of its environment. There is less pressure and more authenticity. In an environment of grace, you are allowed to make mistakes—and even fail. You can admit what you don't know. You can be on a learning curve. It is expected that at some point you will fall short because it is what we as humans do.

Grace doesn't guarantee freedom from relational pain. We all make mistakes that can cause deep harm. People fail. People sin. Christians fail. Christians sin. Christians hurt one another. When love is the motive for relational interactions, rather than performance, we can move toward one another in grace after experiencing hurt—inviting forgiveness, repentance, and reconciliation.

An environment of gracious acceptance can happen anywhere: in a friendship, a small group, a team at work, a family, a study group at college, a schoolroom, or a church. We remember those places where we've experienced this, even if it is with one person. I could not receive the gifts of these grace-filled relationships when I had my wall up, but looking back, many friends and even a few relatives loved and accepted me long before I recognized it.

Performing for Acceptance

Robert McGee, in his book *Search for Significance*, said, "When we base our security on success and others' opinions, we become dependent on our abilities to perform and please others."[13] Performing to be accepted, one of my fig leaves, was a familiar expression of my driven perfectionism. Since people might leave me if they learned what was true about me, I'd better make it worthwhile for them to stay. In doing so, I put myself on a trajectory to crash into reality. I could never do enough to keep everyone happy with me.

Other times I did the opposite. To cope with my fear of being rejected, I tried to ignore my desire to belong. Deep down I wanted to have a place where I was known and celebrated for who I was, and not what I could accomplish. If I had no expectations of anyone asking me to join them or be their friend, I wouldn't be disappointed and feel the shame of their rejection. I played this ping pong game in my mind. Be self-sufficient, don't get your hopes up that people will pursue you, and work hard to gain approval and inclusion. It was a confusing scheme that didn't work.

Within the first year of attending my church, I had two different elders on separate occasions personally welcome me. Both kind men said, "Louise, we care more about who you are than what you do for our church." Though I offered a polite thanks, I thought, *Yeah, right. I'll believe it when I see it.* I assumed I would always be an outsider, never a part of the close-knit community the longtime members had.

For three years I taught the little ones in Sunday school every week. The two women who wrote the preschool curriculum with me were equally committed, and we implemented the material with joy. We had a marvelous time serving and had several other parents join us in the journey. After those years, I was tired. I taught preschool in my job five days a week, I led preschoolers again on Sundays, and my daughters were in preschool. I needed a break from small children.

I gathered my courage and went to the children's pastor to tell him I would like to move to an older group of children. I expected him to be frustrated with me, disappointed I was bailing on him. Instead, he responded, "Okay. That would be great." I was proud that I spoke up for myself, but even more, I was surprised he was agreeable with the idea of me serving in a way that made better sense for me. I didn't know it was possible for this to happen in a church. Could it be that in this church I could admit my limitations?

The Performance Test

Then, the big test happened. My friend, Larry, who served in preschool ministries with me along with his wife, Shasteen, called to ask me to babysit for their two children. Preschool children. I had no other plans that day and I am not a good liar, so I needed to tell him the truth. I took one of the biggest risks of my life. I said, "Larry, I hope you know how much I love your kids, but I am so weary of teaching preschoolers all week and then again on Sundays while my own kids are preschoolers. I don't think I can do it. I know I don't have the energy for watching kids again. I am going to tell you no."

To my amazement, Larry responded, "Okay. I understand. No problem. I'll see you tomorrow in church."

I sat there on my couch in stunned disbelief, with the phone receiver still in my hand. He wasn't mad at me. He didn't judge me. He didn't guilt trip me. He received the acknowledgment of my limitation in stride.

At that moment, a new way of life began for me. My relationship with Larry and Shasteen didn't change. They are two of my closest friends in the world to this day. What changed was that I experienced for the first time that I could be accepted without performing. Larry's response to me began to break down the prison walls of my self-protective striving. It freed me to begin to believe I could be a finite human being and remain valued.

When we know we are forgiven, redeemed, and justified because of Jesus, we are given the opportunity to rest in those truths. The leaders of our church sought to create a gracious climate for me and others so we could practice that rest. A grace-filled relationship allows a person to admit their failings because their sin doesn't define them. Instead, Christ in us defines us as believers. The work of sanctification is a lifelong journey. Grace understands the slow pace of growth and gives space and safety to learn.

When a faith community doesn't know how to give and receive God's grace, it becomes unsafe. It can, without intention, become a shame-based environment where believers have a hard time learning to trust. Sandra Wilson, in her book *Released from Shame,* said it well: "In shame-based religious systems, expectations of participants don't match the truth of spiritual growth and human imperfection."[14]

Honesty about My Struggles

For me to experience spiritual growth, I had to feel free to confess my internal struggles of faith. I also needed a safe place to tell the truth about my sin and the effects of sin in me. Hiding behind my imaginary wall and posturing with my fig leaves left me immature in faith. I needed to take off the old way of doing the Christian life and put on the new way: the new covenant life of grace.

It humbled me to admit what I hid behind my walls and under my fig leaves. Saying aloud what was true about my spiritual immaturity and my shame-based actions felt vulnerable. I was embarrassed to name how I affected my family. I understood the temptation to avoid it by pretending it didn't exist.

"Bypassed shame" is lethal to the process of healing. It compounds the problem because shame thrives in hiddenness. I learned in my 12-step group that any person or group who lives in this denial is practicing the no-talk rule: "No, we're all fine. I come from a wonderful family. Yes, my dad left us for another woman when I was small, but it didn't affect any of us." "Don't talk about that. Don't share our family business in public."

Grace frees us to come out of hiding and declare what is true about what we've done or what happened to us. As I acknowledged my fears, shame, character defects, and immaturity, I observed that my friends at church grew to trust me more. Honesty about my weaknesses revealed my humility before God. This humility drew their respect and love. They responded with grace because they were aware of their own limitations and weren't afraid of mine. As grateful receivers of God's grace, they willingly extended it to me. We were all slowly learning about Jesus and His grace. In the process we sometimes hurt one another, but our desire was to live out Colossians 3:12: "Therefore, as God's chosen people, holy and dearly loved, clothe yourselves with compassion, kindness, humility, gentleness and patience."

Before I came to my new church, I had never been in such an environment. The surroundings I'd experienced before were performance or shame based. I, in turn, created that kind of experience for my family. I didn't know another way. We pass on to others what we know until we learn something different. "We . . . cannot give direction to others struggling with sin when we are trapped in our own," said authors Bill Thrall, Bruce McNicol, and John Lynch in their book *Behind the Mask*.[15] I couldn't be a grace giver until I experienced it myself.

Known and Accepted

As I began to share some of my story with others in our church, one of my fears was that I would be labeled in a way I didn't want. I wanted to be Louise, with all my strengths and weaknesses, like everyone else. When friends trusted what God's Word says about us as believers, I discovered that they saw me as Christ in Louise, not as "the woman from severe abuse." Even when my overreactions to someone brushing past my yet unhealed shame wound were noticed, I was loved and received. They seemed to see past the brokenness to who I really was. It was a great gift to be accepted and embraced while I was immature and messy. They gave me grace and protected my heart. In this church there were imperfect but grace-filled people all around me. It took time for me to rely on that grace and trust them. I vacillated between performance and rest.

Through the shepherding of our elders, I began to have a new experience and understanding of leadership. These men didn't have any interest in controlling me. They seemed to want to protect and celebrate me. I didn't know what to do with their sincere kindness and personal care. It felt refreshing, but I had no idea how to relax and be myself when I was with them. I didn't understand how to receive healthy leadership.

How do you let someone care for you and lead you when their motive is to love you? It was new for me.

Little by little I learned to receive it. I began to understand that God's original design for authority is a good thing. My skepticism of authority, especially male authority, started to decrease. I learned that if authority functions in the protective and for-you loving way it was meant to function, it strengthens and helps mature you into your God-given design.

Hope of Redemption

Rick and Nancy taught me truth and showed me how to live this life of grace. They invested in me for many years as they did with count-less others. At the time I assumed their single intention was to help me heal. I didn't foresee that they, while mentoring me, modeled for me how to be a grace-based leader. Their skill in pastoral counseling combined with their commitment to me demonstrated what healthy discipleship can look like. I acquired more from them than I realized.

During another of my meetings with Rick, we went for a walk. As we moseyed along, I expressed my gratitude to him for his help. I told him what a gift from God he was to me, then listed many ways God was using him in my life.

He thanked me and followed with words I will never forget. "There will be a day, Louise, when you will do what I'm doing."

Astonished, I thought, *How could Rick proclaim those words while I am immature and still need so much healing?* I couldn't imagine helping people as he did, but the thought of it ignited something in my spirit. He recognized a strength and gifting within me I didn't know existed. Because he defined me by who I am in Christ, he could see past my brokenness and discern some of my design. His words gave me hope for a future with meaning and purpose. There could be redemption from my past. I might experience joy in giving away what he, Nancy, and others had given to me.

Dale and Juanita Ryan wrote in *Rooted in God's Love,* "We can let go of our shame when we allow ourselves to remember that God has plans for us that include joy. We are not aimlessly adrift in life, headed nowhere, wanderers in a meaningless maze. On the contrary, every day takes us closer to the fulfillment of God's purposes. Jesus's followers share his conviction that joy, not shame, is God's purpose in creation. . . . We can remind ourselves that God's plans for us include joy."[16] With Rick's words of encouragement, I could look to the future and begin to dream of the beauty in store for me. Whether Rick was accurate in his assessment of my potential or not, I knew God was in the process of redeeming me for His glory.

When I asked God to guide me to a place where I could be shown a new way to live the Christian life, one that brought hope and true help, I had no idea of the enormity of the change that new place would bring me. We sometimes forget that God hears and remembers every cry of our hearts, even when we don't recall them. He answers above and beyond anything we can ask or imagine (Eph. 3:20).

In this church, God slowly transformed me by showing me how to live in His grace instead of through performance. As I learned, He healed and equipped me. I could not have believed it was possible in the beginning, but in His perfect time, God did release me to do the very thing Rick said I would do. It was a miracle of His grace.

Chapter 7

BITTERNESS TO JOY

As months passed and I continued to meet with both Rick and Nancy regularly, I learned to submit to their counsel, even when it was hard. I wanted the dysfunction from my childhood to harm my family as little as possible. I was driven to do everything I could, as quickly as I could, to heal for their sake. Support groups, counseling, and many books about healing from childhood abuse encouraged my growth and began to shape a new way of life for me. I loved the hope that my past didn't define me and that I could live in the design of who God created me to be.

God's Plan Versus My Plan

As I grew in strength of self-worth, my desire for justice increased. I dreamed of confronting my parents about the abuse. Confrontation to me was an avenue to expose them. God's heart in unresolved relational sin is for reconciliation. I knew this from 2 Corinthians 5:18: "All this is from God, who reconciled us to himself through Christ and gave us the ministry of reconciliation." I wasn't there yet. My motive was not to reconcile with them. I wanted revenge.

In truth, I remained terrified of my parents and trembled at the thought of being in the same room with either of them. I wasn't ready. The biggest hurdle was that I needed to forgive them before I met with them. Rick committed to be there with me when I confronted my parents, but only after I had forgiven them.

What? Forgive them? They didn't deserve forgiveness. They deserved judgment and condemnation. I thought hell was not a fitting enough ending place for them. The biblical injunction was correct, but I had zero interest in doing it.

"It is important that you forgive your parents from your heart, Louise," Rick said. "We do this because God has asked us to. But also, if you don't forgive, when we confront them, your parents will see it. They will have power over you because they inherently know that the power of sin is greater than the power of Louise. They will not respond well, it will inflame your shame, and your response will be unhealthy. The meeting will look like it is about you and not about the sin in them."

Because my parents claim to be Christians, it was important that I followed Scripture's directives on how to deal with unaddressed sin in relationships. Jesus taught this in Matthew 18:15–17: "If your brother sins against you, go and show him his fault, just between the two of you. If he listens to you, you have won your brother over. But if he will not listen, take one or two others along, so that every matter may be established by the testimony of two or three witnesses. If he refuses to listen even to them, tell it to the church; and if he refuses to listen even to the church, treat him as you would a pagan or a tax collector."

Learning to Forgive

What was I to do? If forgiving them would help me to expose them, then that was what I would have to do. I had no reasonable idea of how to do it, having never forgiven anyone before in my life. I had been a Christian for thirty years and could quote verses on forgiveness, but

I had never forgiven. I didn't know how. How does a person forgive? Speaking the words, "I forgive you," accomplishes nothing while still holding onto the hurt. I knew Jesus asked us to forgive, but I believed my offenders wouldn't admit culpability, so I felt trapped in the wait for justice. A debt must be paid, and a debt must be released, but saying the words doesn't mean you let it go.

Rick encouraged me to take a step toward forgiveness by naming what happened to me, by creating a list of how my parents harmed me. The list was to include how my parents injured me as well as the effects of those trespasses against me. Forgiving for the sins alone is not complete. We must also forgive the effects or the consequences of the sin on us. I knew the list would be extensive, so I began the process right away.

I found a new spiral notebook in a drawer and began writing. The list went on until the notebook was almost filled. It was a cathartic experience to write it. I filled many pages on the day I first started the list and kept the notebook with me in the weeks that followed. As I thought of more wrongs or more effects and consequences, I added them. I kept this up until I could think of nothing more to write that hadn't already been recorded. Seeing on paper what I had been carrying all those years was helpful. It made sense that I felt as I did about myself, about my parents, and about life. No wonder I felt angry and bitter.

Seeing all I had written grieved me. I cried over what happened to me. No one deserves what I experienced. I could see myself with compassion, knowing this truth. My sadness over what happened to me was important to my process. Some have only ever been sad about what has happened to them yet need to feel their anger. For me, I had been angry so long, it was critical to be sad. I needed to experience the full breadth of my emotions so my forgiveness lacked nothing. Full emotional understanding and expression frees forgiveness.

Wrestling with God

The next step was to release my parents from the debt I believed they owed me. I needed to let it go. How would I get to a place of release? I didn't relish the idea of forgiving my parents, but I knew it had to be done.

I sat on the couch in my family room, wrestling with God. "I don't want to do this, God. I know I am supposed to forgive, but I want You to know the only reason I am doing this is because I have to. There is nothing in me that desires this. I understand this reveals how immature and unchristlike I am, but it is the truth. I do *not* want to forgive them. I want them to suffer for what they did."

I picked up the spiral notebook, walked into my bedroom, knelt beside my bed, opened to my list, and tried saying the words. Silence.

"God, I need to forgive my father for what he did to me."

My heart refused. I closed the spiral notebook and walked away.

Another day I tried again, and my response remained the same. I had no desire to forgive. I didn't want to let my parents off the hook for what they had done.

Again and again I knelt by my bed with my spiral notebook open and my heart closed. You can't move forward when your heels are dug in, and I liked right where my heels were. I thought since I was in the right, I shouldn't have to do this. They should be coming to me groveling in remorse for what they did. I shouldn't have to release them from the debt they owed me. They should apologize first. Then—and only then— might I consider forgiving them for what they owed me.

I knew nothing would change unless God helped me. I began to pray. "God, help me to be willing ... to be willing ... to be willing ... to forgive my parents." Two *willings* were not enough. I wasn't willing, nor was I willing to *be* willing. I had to ask for three *willings*. I needed God's help to be willing to be willing to be willing to forgive.

The days and months went by, and I kept praying this prayer, this three-times-willing prayer, each time with the same result. All my driven effort to move the process along was rendered useless because my heart, mind, and will remained stubborn. I didn't want to do it. I knelt by my bed and laid my spiral notebook on the peach-colored down comforter next to the hunter green pillow shams. I opened it to number 1 on the list of harms and inevitably got nowhere.

"God, help me." Silence. "I need to forgive my father for what he did to me. ARGH! I don't want to!" I slammed the notebook shut and threw it across the room. I don't know how many times I tried, but I couldn't will my hardened heart to obey. I was at a standstill.

Hooks in My Heart

One morning at church, while walking up the stairs to the preschool Sunday school room, I thought about the list in my spiral notebook. I was frustrated and angry at what I believed was the injustice of it all. Why should I be the miserable one? *They* should be suffering from the guilt of their sin—not me. I was in Phoenix with a list of harms done to me that I carried in my mind and heart. My parents were living their lives hundreds of miles away, oblivious to the damage they created, walking around scot-free. Something was amiss.

A picture of cable wire came to mind—a strong, thick metal wire twisted like rope. At the end of the cable wire was a hook, and that hook was embedded deep in my heart. Then I saw a cable wire with a hook for each of the harms listed in my spiral notebook. The hooks were mangled together, maneuvering for space in my heart. It's a wonder there was room for anything else. The other end of the wire was in my parents' home. I walked around doing life with hooks in my heart, dismal and broken, and my parents were miles away, living happily in their delusion of innocence.

I began to live with a constant awareness of the presence of these hooks in my heart, and I wanted them gone. It wasn't fair that I should be the one carrying the pain and shame of what happened to me because of their sinful selfishness. What if they never admitted their guilt? What if they never apologized? Why should I have to be the one to pay for what they did? I carried the pain, shame, and consequences of their trespasses against me. It is no surprise this revelation angered me.

I wanted to be released from the anguish and burden I carried. I needed to be free of the hooks in my heart. I began to understand the need to forgive my parents for *my* sake. I certainly wasn't ready to forgive my parents for their sake so they might possibly repent of what they did, enabling reconciliation. I needed to forgive only because of *my* need for it.

I knelt by my bed and opened my spiral notebook. Once more I tried to say the words about forgiving my father for what he did to me. I pretended to take one of the figurative hooks out of my heart while I said the words. It didn't help.

"No! I don't want to forgive them, even for my sake. It is wrong what they did!" Again, I slammed the notebook shut and threw it across the room. I despaired that I would ever be able to release them from the debt they owed me.

Saying the Words

Soon, I tried again. I sighed deeply, asking God to do what only He could do in me. By this time, my heart was humbler, feeling the desperation of what I could not do apart from Christ in me. I opened my notebook, pretended to take the hook for number 1 on my list out of my heart, and I said the words.

"God, I choose to forgive my father—" Silence. I couldn't let go of the hook. I didn't want to let go of the hook.

"Help me give this back to my dad, God. Let's try again. God, I choose to forgive my father—" I took a deep breath, still holding onto the hook. I felt the familiar powerlessness arise. I needed God's help.

"No! I can't, God! I want him to pay for what he did. I want him to pay! Maybe I need to give the hook to You, God, so You can help me to forgive."

I turned from where I imagined my dad to be in the room to where I imagined God to be in the room. "God, I am giving You this hook. Help me to forgive my father. . . . NO! I will not forgive him. I want him to pay! *Someone has to pay!*"

And then it came to me. Jesus paid. Jesus paid for what my father did to me.

Tears ran down my cheeks as the Holy Spirit brought Colossians 3:13 to my mind: "Forgive as the Lord forgave you."

In that instant, I remembered that my sin nailed Jesus to the cross as much as my parents' sin nailed Jesus to the cross. I was not more righteous than they were. I was guilty before God too. I had no right to judge them or withhold forgiveness from them. My parents and I stood on level ground in front of the cross. I understood that Jesus paid for my parents' sin against me so I could be free. I no longer needed to hold onto the hooks and wait for my parents to pay for what they did to me. They could never pay for it. Only Jesus could and did. Oh, what love Jesus has for us!

In recognizing God's forgiveness for me, how could I withhold the same from my parents? I had been stuck in unforgiveness because I placed myself above my parents in judgment of them. At the foot of the cross, I learned that I must step off the self-righteous judgment seat before I can forgive. Though my sins looked different from my parents', we all needed Someone who could save us from our sin, and that Someone was Jesus. His perfect atoning sacrifice paid our debt.

In that newfound awareness, I went down through the list in my spiral notebook, releasing my parents from the debt they owed me, in about ten minutes. I let it all go. The hooks were gone. I had never before experienced such joy. The shame of all they had done to me and what I carried because of their sin against me lifted away.

Released from Debt

Because Jesus paid the price for our sin *and* the sin others have done to us, we can be free. He paid the debt we and those who hurt us cannot pay. The atonement Jesus accomplished for us at the cross is not a theory or meaningless history. It is real and is meant to release us from sin's devastation. Sin is where shame has its power, therefore forgiveness heals our shame because it releases us from the effects of sin.

Jesus said, "Forgive, and you will be forgiven" (Luke 6:37). This Greek word for *forgive* is *apoluo*, which means "release." He said, "Release, and you will be released." Without forgiveness, without release, we are held captive to the sin and the debt created by it. Knowing the debt is paid, we can let it go because the transaction is complete. Justice has been meted out. What was owed us or what we owe is covered by Jesus's blood. God invites us to believe and trust that He has accomplished this for us. In this decision, we humble our hearts before the only true and righteous judge so we can be released and release others from the debt we attempt to carry on our own.

Jesus's last words on the cross were, "It is finished" (John 19:30). The demonstration of His great love, mercy, and grace are revealed in these final words before He died. He spoke those words for our sake. He completed the work of healing for us. It was done. David Seamands said, in his book *Healing for Damaged Emotions*, "In the cross, God demonstrated His total identification with us in *our undeserved suffer-ing*, as well as *our deserved punishment*. . . . On the cross, God in Christ has absorbed all these kinds of painful feelings into His love. They have entered into His heart, pierced His soul, and been dissolved in the ocean of His forgiveness and the sea of His forgetfulness."[17] We cannot absorb the effects of sin into us, but Jesus can, and He did at the cross.

The miracle of forgiveness frees me from shame. In giving or receiv-ing forgiveness, God's grace, mercy, and great love overcome my shame, and I see myself and others with clarity. I am free to then offer that gift of forgiveness to my offenders. Only He could pay the debt we could not pay. The sins my parents committed against me were nailed to the cross, and atonement was completed.

Hallelujah

I learned as I forgave my parents that I didn't need my parents' confession and apology for me to be free. Jesus did that work for me. I needed their confession and apology for reconciliation to happen and for trust to begin to be rebuilt, but I didn't need it to heal from the pain of what they did. Nor did I need it to heal from my shame. Lewis B. Smedes noted in his book *Shame and Grace*, "When we genuinely forgive, we set a prisoner free and then discover that the prisoner we set free was us."[18]

My favorite hymn is "It Is Well with My Soul" by Horatio G. Spafford, written after he lost his entire family at sea. In the time of his darkest grief, he worshiped God for what the atonement wrought for him.

> My sin—oh, the bliss of this glorious thought!—
> My sin, not in part but the whole,
> Is nailed to the cross, and I bear it no more,
> Praise the Lord, praise the Lord, O my soul!

Refrain:

It is well with my soul,

It is well, it is well with my soul.[19]

Not just my sin, but my parents' sin and the sin of the whole world, not in part but the whole, is nailed to the cross. We bear it and the resulting shame no more if we choose to receive God's forgiveness and offer it to others. My parents carry full responsibility before God for what they have done. If they never own that responsibility and never apologize or express remorse for their abuse, their sins are still borne by Jesus at the cross. I can be free by releasing them from the debt they owe me. I can forgive them because Jesus paid it all. *Hallelujah!* It is well, it is well with my soul.

Chapter 8

Offers of Reconciliation

Forgiveness is a miracle of God. He answered my three-times-willing prayer above and beyond anything I could ask or imagine. Through forgiveness, God unchained me from of the prison of my bitterness. My heart felt lighter, free of the hooks that mutilated it for decades. Dignity was restored through Jesus paying the debt my parents owed me. Desire for vengeance vanished. Jesus's love expressed through the cross fulfilled justice for the wrong done to me. Releasing my parents from their debt was a giant step toward healing from shame.

My thoughts shifted regarding meeting with my parents to offer them a chance to repent and reconcile. My motive was no longer to expose them. I was ready to stand beside them in front of the cross, hand in hand, pointing them to the One who could bring life and healing. Yet I still feared. My fears changed from terror for my life to the anticipation of the hard work required if my parents did repent and desire to reconcile. I didn't trust them, nor did I feel safe with them. Forgiving them didn't restore the broken trust.

Possibilities Ahead

As I prepared for the trip across the country, Rick's wise counsel helped ready me for the confrontation with my parents. He advised me to create a list of all potential responses from them. How might they react to me bringing their abuse to the light? I needed to be prepared emotionally and spiritually for any possibility. My list included these heavy scenarios:

1. They will deny it.

2. They will say I am making it up.

3. They will say I am exaggerating.

4. They will try to kill me.

5. They will try to kill themselves.

6. They will spread lies about me.

7. They will apologize and repent.

It was critical to determine a healthy response to each scenario. This was a sobering but helpful process. The most challenging possibility for me was the last one. The thought of trying to build a healthy relationship with my parents overwhelmed me. If they repented, I would have a new kind of relationship with them, but that seemed impossible. I would need help with that process should they humble their hearts before me.

I committed to follow Jesus's steps toward reconciliation from Matthew 18. I prepared documents to guide the discussion with my parents, including a list of their abuses against me and a letter to read to them. I wanted to share my forgiveness and hope for reconciliation. I prayed that the words I wrote would be used of God to soften their hearts and encourage them to repent.

Greater Love

The week before we left to fly to my parents' city, Chuck and I met with Rick one last time to go over details. Rick gave me a final instruction. "Louise, before we go, I want you to make sure your affairs are in order. I think there is a good chance your father will try to kill you for bringing exposure to his crimes."

I gulped and nodded in agreement. I knew what my father was capable of.

Rick added, "I want you to know I have put my affairs in order, because I think there is a good chance that your father may also try to kill me."

What passed through my mind at that moment, and in every recollection of that moment, is this verse: "Greater love has no one than this, that he lay down his life for his friends" (John 15:13). My pastor was willing to lay down his life for me. Such courage, love, and faithfulness. I had never known protection like that before. It was perhaps one of the greatest expressions of love I will experience in this life. His willingness to protect me gave me strength for what was ahead. The possible danger we were to face created legitimate fear. We needed God's covering. Several people committed to pray for God's protection over us as we met with my parents.

Scriptural Encouragement

In the days leading up to our first trip, sleep eluded me. I looked at our beautiful daughters and prayed for their security. I held them close, feeling vulnerable and afraid. I knew that courage was not the absence of fear, but the choice to walk through the fear to do what needed to be done. I had to do this. I had to bring the sin to the light for all our sakes.

I kept a Bible verse calendar near my kitchen sink for daily encouragement. Looking for strength, I read ahead to the verses for the days we were to be gone. It's comforting how God meets us in small and big ways through our steps of faith and obedience. On the day we were to fly to our destination, the verse on the calendar said: "Have no fear of sudden disaster or of the ruin that overtakes the wicked, for the Lord will be your confidence and will keep your foot from being snared" (Prov. 3:25–26). The day we were to meet with my parents, the verse on the calendar said: "Don't be afraid! Speak out! Don't quit! For I am with you and no one can harm you" (Acts 18:9–10 TLB).

I received these words as promises from God. I needed reassurance of God's presence as we faced my parents. I needed His peace in my fear and His hope for the future. God's grace to me was profound in my need.

Two Trips

At the meeting, Chuck and I sat with my parents, a representative from their church, and Rick. Sitting across the table from my parents, I felt the heaviness and vulnerability of the moment. I looked them in the eyes, feeling strong and ready to share what I had prepared. Still, I felt sad that this meeting needed to happen. God's powerful presence of protection and peace filled the room. In answer to prayer, I experienced nominal fear. I read my documents and waited quietly for their response. They offered no admittance of guilt. I was grieved but not surprised by their denial. Taking responsibility for their abuse would have created significant consequences in their lives.

As we left, the intensity of the experience made my ears ring. I was glad to be alive and grateful for God's faithfulness to the promises He gave me from my kitchen Scripture calendar. God kept us from harm.

Before we boarded the plane back to Phoenix, Rick said, "I can think of less than a handful of times in my life when I have tangibly felt the presence and protection of the Lord. This was one of those times."

Rick, Chuck, and I played cards on the plane, but I couldn't focus. The meeting with my parents replayed like a video recording in my mind. The adrenaline rush that resulted from the need for acute concentration kept me awake for a few days.

Over a year later, Rick and another elder from our church went with us to meet with my parents a second time in obedience to Jesus's words in Matthew. We brought the witness of my sister. Her terror of my father prevented her presence at the meeting, so she wrote out her testimony and sent it with her husband to read in her stead.

My parents remained in denial of wrongdoing and expressed no desire to reconcile. Much like after the first meeting, I was saddened but not shocked. The cost for repentance would be high for them. Once again, God delivered us from all harm. His powerful presence covered us.

As we drove away from their church, the ear-ringing adrenaline rush appeared again, as it had after the first meeting. My parent's choice to self-protect rather than humble themselves before me and my sister pierced my heart. Still, I did what God asked me to do, and in this I felt peace.

Though my parents didn't confess their guilt, these attempts at reconciliation brought healing to my shame. Confronting my parents for their abuse produced self-respect in me and strengthened my spirit. I discovered that I could speak up and be heard, even if my parents denied their abuse. I knew I had reported the truth. The decision of my pastor and another elder of my church to stand in my defense shed new light on my value. It told me that they believed me and were willing to fight for me. Their actions communicated that I was worth their effort. I am forever grateful for their sacrificial love and protection.

Returning Home

One would think that returning home from two powerful times of experiencing God's presence in danger might free me to trust God without reservation. It didn't. Though I witnessed incredible spiritual and physical protection during both trips, afterward, the memory of the safety rattled me.

Yes, God shielded me, but why did He protect in these instances and not at other times? He is Almighty God. He can do anything. If He loves me, why did He allow the abuse in my childhood? Is He capricious? Does He deliver only when it suits Him? I could see no rhyme or reason in His plan. It left me confused and full of shame, certain that the problem was me.

A friend told me early in my healing journey that God wanted me to be a trophy of His grace. At the time the statement angered me. I didn't want to be a trophy of God's grace. I wanted the abuse I experienced to not have happened. I wanted to be a cherished child of God instead of feeling like a pawn on His giant chess board. I wanted to be something besides my shame self. I couldn't shake the gratitude I felt for God's covering during the meetings with my parents, but I needed greater understanding of who He is and His personal care for me in order to heal. God remained faithful to continue to teach me.

Open for Reconciliation

Thirty years have passed since the first meeting, and my parents have not contacted the elders of our church, which was the first step we requested if they desired to reconcile. I don't know why they have remained silent. I can only speculate as to their reasons. The door remains open for reconciliation if they so choose.

If they ever become willing to reconcile, they would need to admit what they did, apologize, and then receive professional counseling to help them understand why they harmed us as they did. They would need to grasp how the abuse affected my sister and me. Then and only then could a journey toward building trust begin. If they humbled their hearts and truly repented, reconciliation would be possible—even if it took many years. Luke 17:3 says, "If your brother sins, rebuke him, and if he repents, forgive him." God's way, even in the most challenging circumstances, is that we forgive and reconcile when a sinner repents.

Confrontations for severe abuse must be handled with wisdom and great care. I was able to meet with my parents because I had been prepared well and was ready for the interaction. I had tremendous support from experienced leaders who knew how to guide the process. They were ready to step in and halt the meeting if there was a possibility of re-abuse. These trained and trusted protectors are vital for any attempt at reconciliation in these circumstances.

It would have been impossible to offer reconciliation to my parents before I forgave them. When I forgave, the sting and shame of the abuse lessened. The debt for their wrongs was paid and justice was meted out by Jesus's substitutionary death. These miraculous gifts of God through the cross free us. But I didn't forget what my parents did. Trust was not restored after I forgave. Trust needed to be earned. If we were confident of my parents' repentance and they followed through with the necessary steps to earn my trust, then it would be my journey to risk beginning a new relationship with them.

Without the power of the Holy Spirit in me to take the first step of reconciliation, I am confident I couldn't have done it. With the Holy Spirit's power, it is doable. It is His work in us, and He calls us to it. "Therefore, if anyone is in Christ, he is a new creation; the old has gone, the new has come! All this is from God, who reconciled us to himself through Christ and gave us the ministry of reconciliation: that God was reconciling the world to himself in Christ, not counting men's sins against them. And he has committed to us the message of reconciliation" (2 Cor. 5:17–19).

We can respond to our offenders with grace, knowing we stand on level ground with them in front of the cross. The one who harmed us is no longer our enemy, but our fellow human, in need of a Savior. In this posture of humility, we depend on the Holy Spirit for strength to risk a renewed relationship with the one who hurt us. God asks us to do this and gives us the grace and power to trust Him through it. He can do in us what we cannot do. It is the good news of the gospel. Nothing is impossible with God. His work to free me to forgive and attempt to reconcile with my parents bore witness to that reality. The transforming work of the Holy Spirit is real. Every day I looked more like that trophy of God's grace and less like my shame self. The miracles of healing continued.

Chapter 9

Unbelief and Shame

With every obstacle lifted from the path of healing, a new one emerged. It perplexed me that my journey of healing from the effects of my childhood dragged on. I couldn't deny change and even miracles had occurred, but I was far from feeling whole. I still had a long way to go, which brought discouragement and frustration. When would I be finished with the process? Life was not going according to plan, at least not *my* plan. If God was my healer, what took Him so long?

The mountain of issues that remained to be addressed daunted me. It would take years for the needed healing. When I gave my life to God at junior high camp, telling Him I wanted Him to use me in big ways for His kingdom, I imagined something more like Billy Graham: a life of exciting and life-giving ministry. I despised the reality that I gave my life to Jesus and was spending my thirties dealing with the mess handed down to me from my parents. This was not what I signed up for. I didn't want it. I wanted a purpose that made me feel good about myself, not a process that regularly revealed my inadequacies.

I didn't fully recognize God's gradual and continual work in me. Shame alleged that He paid attention only when it was convenient.

Mistrust in God and His regard for me began to rule my thoughts. Shame and unbelief were so tangled in my heart and mind that I couldn't discern where one ended and the other began. The part of me that was still growing out of childhood pain needed time to learn to trust.

Doubting My Faith

I reflected on my interactions with God. I didn't understand His ways. I didn't know how to make Him happy. Striving hadn't worked. I continued to feel distant from Him. I became bolder and more honest about doubting my faith. I pondered Bible verses I knew since childhood and could not validate their message based upon my experience.

> You are my hiding place;
>> you will protect me from trouble
>> and surround me with songs of deliverance. (Ps. 32:7)
>
> The Lord will keep you from all harm—
>> he will watch over your life. (Ps. 121:7)
>
> And my God will meet all your needs according to his glorious riches in Christ Jesus. (Phil. 4:19)
>
> God is our refuge and strength,
>> an ever-present help in trouble. (Ps. 46:1)
>
> The Lord is faithful to all his promises
>> and loving toward all he has made. (Ps. 145:13)

After careful analysis, I determined that God did not do what these verses said. Therefore, in my case, they were not true. I didn't believe them. If He didn't come through in my childhood, what good were the promises to me now? Shame eclipsed my faith.

I was relieved to read about Moses, a giant of the faith who also struggled to believe God because of shame. I was not the only one. When God spoke to Moses in the burning bush, telling him he was to lead Israel, Moses responded in unbelief. He spoke of his unworthiness:

"Moses said to the Lord, 'O Lord, I have never been eloquent, neither in the past nor since you have spoken to your servant. I am slow of speech and tongue'" (Exod. 4:10). Moses's shame-filled self-assessment kept him from believing God. *Just like me.*

I read books about great Christians who experienced miraculous deliverance by God, and I believed them. God is all-powerful and can do anything. He can be a help in trouble. Friends who didn't know of my internal battle commended me for my great faith. In response, I said I believed God for others but not for me. Since He delivered others and He didn't deliver me as a child, the problem must be me. My conclusion was He comes through for people He likes, or the ones who have done enough good and deserve His help.

Unanswered Prayer

Years of unanswered prayer brought more struggle. God said no to prayers when I thought He should have said yes—if He was faithful to His Word. The verses that speak of God's promises were not what I experienced. How could I believe Him? Was God teasing me like a taunting older brother?

> Ask and it will be given to you; seek and you will find; knock and the door will be opened to you. (Matt. 7:7)
> He will call upon me, and I will answer him;
>> I will be with him in trouble,
>> I will deliver him and honor him. (Ps. 91:15)

I asked. I called upon Him. I prayed for God to help me as a wife and a mother—the most important thing in life to me. Instead of creating a beautiful family and home, I felt clueless and seemed to regularly fail. He didn't open the door to me. He didn't deliver me or honor me. All my efforts seemed to fall flat or never be enough.

Even after I lay prostrate on the floor, begging God to help me, I continued to make mistakes that hurt our family. My woundedness and emotional immaturity that resulted from the abuse of my childhood wreaked havoc in my home. My children grew up quicker than my healing process could manage. They needed me to be more mature than I was, and no matter how hard I tried to work on my issues, I seemed to lag behind on what they needed from me. My shame told me I should never have been a mother. God made a mistake.

Shame, combined with my unbelief in God's personal care for me, created a deficit. If I didn't believe God would take care of me, a new system was required. Since I couldn't depend on God, I needed a fallback plan for protecting me and my children. Instead of God, the protector would have to be me. I thought this was an excellent strategy. *I can do this.*

I was hypervigilant in hovering over my children. Parenting routines for me were borne out of fear and shame. Did I mother in the right way? Did I create enough good memories? Did I help them enough but not too much? Should I arrange playdates more often for them? What should I do if they won't eat their vegetables? What chores were appropriate for them? I had no idea. Relaxing and enjoying my children meant I wasn't diligent enough. I went to bed exhausted every night from the effort.

I did everything I could to be self-sufficient. I managed our household, cooked, cleaned, made sure everything ran well, and worked outside the home to help pay bills. I perceived myself to be the lone disciplining parent and the one who did most of the work, even though I didn't trust my husband to try. If I wasn't in control, then the girls and I would be unprotected and hurt. It was a no-win situation for us both. My shame-and-unbelief-based plan for managing life without God faltered.

Scolded by Shame

Then it happened. We were at the park one day with friends. I sat chatting with my girlfriend while our kids climbed on the playground equipment. Rachel, my youngest, was next to me digging in the sand. Emily, my oldest, was on the monkey bars, out of my reach. Emily was a champ on the monkey bars and had great upper body strength, built by her years on the preschool playground where I worked. That day, Emily lost traction and fell to the sandy ground, landing on her chin and splitting it open, creating a bloody mess.

Emily was crying—appropriately—but I was hysterical. I had been found out. The curtain came up, and there I was, standing naked on the stage. I was not the protective mom I needed to be. I had neglected her and not been right there with her while she was on the monkey bars. As a result, she had been harmed. It was *my* fault. I failed.

My girlfriend took us to her nearby house and cleaned the sand from Emily's wound since I was too distraught to do so. It looked like Emily needed stitches, and my friend said we should take her to the emergency room. Then she asked me, "Louise, if you are this upset over Emily needing a few stitches, what will you do if something big happens?"

I knew my friend was right, but I couldn't contain myself.

When Chuck retrieved us to drive to the emergency room, he stated the obvious. "Louise, you're crying harder than Emily is crying. She needs you to take care of her. You're acting like you're hurt worse than she is."

The failure of my plan revealed itself. It exposed my insufficiency to protect my daughter. She was hurt because of my neglect. My shame scolded me that I was no different than my mother. I felt helpless.

Contempt for God

Self-sufficiency and hypervigilant parenting to keep my children from harm missed the mark, but I didn't believe God. What else could I do? Though it didn't accomplish anything, what I did next gave me a sense of satisfaction. I grumbled. I grumbled like the Israelites did in the wilderness when God didn't show up for them in the time or way they wanted. I felt entitled to do it. I sneered, "God sure has a funny way of showing His love. Oh, yes, God loves the whole world, but it is obvious He loves some people more than others. If this is your version of helping, God, then I don't want your help, thank You very much. I'll figure it out for myself."

I complained about our finances. I complained about relational disappointments. I complained that my children didn't have opportunities other children had because we couldn't afford it. I complained we didn't have nice furniture or a dishwasher. I let it be known that my life was harder than everyone else's life. And it wasn't fair.

My contempt for God grew every day, as did my anger toward Him. At the counsel of my mentor, Nancy, I started to journal my thoughts and feelings. I wrote one word on each page in giant letters. "I. AM. MAD. AT. YOU. GOD!" and then walked away. So much for journaling. In time, I learned to write and write and write, pouring my heart out, telling God how unfair I believed Him to be. "If this is protection, then this is a joke!" "If this is your idea of kindness, then what does cruelty look like?" Unbelief was potent in me, as was the shame that fueled it.

Judging God

I knew I resented God, but I didn't realize I had positioned myself as His judge. I became my own god. From my wounded mindset, I thought I knew better than He did. I would have a different plan for the world than He had. I was not humble before Him because I didn't think

He deserved that posture from me. I stood up in my heart against Him, having no desire to kneel before Him and worship Him as my creator and King.

My flesh, the seat of sin in me, wanted to make God what I wanted Him to be. In my younger adult years, I criticized those who created their own version of God, but I did the same thing. I knew friends who shaped God to be only loving and kind, like a gentle uncle who never disciplines but brings money and gifts when he comes to visit.

What I wanted was a God who could be understood and managed. I wanted God to step inside the box I created for Him. I began to understand why some people become atheists. When we can't reconcile our painful life experiences with a loving God, we determine a way to deal with the struggle. I have not yet in my life met anyone who had a different route to atheism than this, even if they offered intellectual arguments.

I knew too many proofs of the validity of God's existence to reject Him. Instead, I continued with my grumbling, my contempt for God, and my desire that He would be who I wanted Him to be. I had no desire to obey Him from my heart. How can you obey from the heart when you don't believe the one you are to obey?

Because I was afraid to dive into full rebellion, I lived in compliance. I jumped through hoops to keep God happy. I performed out of fear of what God would do if I didn't. I rebelled in small ways that made me feel strong. I drove a little more than five miles over the speed limit, and used foul language under my breath, behaviors I wouldn't have dreamed of doing years earlier. If I didn't want to follow the rules, no one could stop me. In my thinking, it dwarfed God, making Him aware I wasn't going to take His disinterest in me laying down. Larry Crabb, in his book *Connections*, said, "Sin is independence, a rebellion against God's authority based on disbelief in his goodness, an independence that creates agendas for our lives that run directly counter to his."[20] I didn't believe in His goodness and enjoyed my independence from Him.

The System of Works

I had attended my church for a few years at this point, a gathering of people who live and breathe the message of God's grace. Learning to embrace grace took longer than I anticipated. The imprint of the previous thirty-two years of a performance-based theology of sanctification (spiritual maturing) left its mark on me. Growing up I learned I was justified (declared righteous) and wore the robe of Jesus's righteousness, but it was only positional before God the Father. I was taught that my heart remained deceitful and desperately wicked, therefore I needed to put forth every effort to grow in holiness. We were taught to share the message of salvation to everyone we knew, even if they didn't want to hear it. Having a quiet time with God every day to know Scripture and doctrine was our task. The more knowledge we had, the better.

I had heard no teaching about developing intimacy or trust in God. That was somehow supposed to happen through duty and obligation. If you checked off all the boxes, you were considered mature. If you didn't check off all the boxes, or worse, if you weren't interested in checking off all the boxes, you were never going to mature. You could be given the label of a carnal or backsliding Christian. The fear placed before us was the question, "When you arrive in heaven, will God say to you, 'Well done, good and faithful servant'?" The thought of being shamed by God in heaven for failing on earth paralyzed me.

Because I gave my life to Jesus as a middle schooler, I had been indoctrinated to the system of works, and it wasn't easy to give up. I hadn't yet learned to trust anyone with me. I wanted to trust God's grace and believe I didn't have to work to earn His love. I didn't know how to stop achieving to keep God happy. Why didn't He stop the abuse

I received unless it was partially my fault? Letting go of performance felt risky.

I believed that the abuse, plus the turmoil in my marriage and my life, were God's punishment for me. I failed and sinned. I was certain of that. At times I forgot to read my Bible every day. Sometimes I was so angry at God I didn't want to pray. I struggled to believe God for who He is and didn't want to share the gospel with anyone, knowing it would be hypocritical to do so. I was tired of dying to self as I had understood it. I wanted to have what I wanted when I wanted it. Brennan Manning, in his book *A Glimpse of Jesus, Stranger to Self-hatred*, quoted what David S. Burns said about the fruit of this legalistic lifestyle: "Legalism creates a mask of conformity which makes the believer holy in his eyes and thus prevents him from coming to self-knowledge. Legalistic religion stresses will-power, and it is this very stress on personal effort that makes the legalist unaware of his real feelings, of his own brokenness, and hence of his need for redemption."[21] Legalism had not matured me. It broke me. It empowered my unbelief. I followed the rules of the law in my own strength, and it stripped me of trust, humility, and healthy dependency, shaming me to my core.

I didn't yet know how to live in relationship with God, except to feel shame in His presence. My shame and unbelief were inextricably linked. The memories of my childhood and the challenging situations I encountered cemented in my mind and heart what I believed in my shame to be true. I continued to see God and my life through the veils of my shame. I concluded that nothing good was going to happen to me because I was worthless and unlovable. God wasn't ever going to drop me a bone because I was not enough. *God, You are not who You say You are. You do not think of me in the way Your Word says You do.* Unbelief was strong in me.

No More Pretending

I ceased pretending about my faith. No more masks. I decided to never feign as if I believed God when I didn't. In choosing authenticity, I healed, but I didn't know it. I didn't realize I was taking off the old way of doing my Christian life one layer at a time. I didn't recognize my growth because I remained unhappy, often in bondage to the lies of my shame and filled with suspicion about God. Weren't maturing Christians supposed to experience joy and peace?

In one of my appointments with Rick, he once again spoke truth in a way I could hear. He said, "Louise, I know you don't believe that God loves you."

I recoiled from him in disbelief. "What? How did you know that? I've never told you that!" Incredulous at his discernment, I added, "Yes, you're right, but how did you know that?"

"It's because you're so full of fear. First John 4:18. First John 4:18! Louise, your life is full of fear." He quoted it for me: "'There is no fear in love. But perfect love drives out fear, because fear has to do with punishment. The one who fears is not made perfect in love.'"

Like many other Scriptures, I heard this familiar passage with new ears. It was true. I was full of fear and didn't believe God loved me. I feared God's punishment if I didn't get everything in life just right. I feared I could never do enough to make God love me. I feared I would fail as a mother. I feared we wouldn't have enough money to pay our bills. I feared I would never feel loved as a wife. I feared I would never amount to anything. I feared. I feared. I feared.

Was it possible to learn to live without fear? Could I ever learn to believe and receive God's love for me? I wanted to know He loved me like it seemed He loved others. Could I know by experience that God loved me? Would God give me eyes to see His love for me if it was true?

Would I be able to really trust Him then? If it was possible, I wanted to learn to live in this way. If I could believe and experience God's love without shame, I knew it would change everything.

Chapter 10

Doubt to Worship

In my youth, most of the Christians I knew seemed guarded, anxious, vigilant, and judgmental toward themselves and others. Many carried hidden sin and fear. Like me. They quoted Scripture, presented the gospel message to strangers and friends, tithed regularly, and served long hours in church each week. When they talked about their personal relationship with God, the words came out almost forced, like they were saying what they thought they *should* say rather than what was true.

"We are struggling with our finances, but we trust God to supply all of our needs," these Christians might say. Yet the expression on their faces belied they were more afraid than trusting. It was as if they were trying to convince themselves as they spoke. It was rare to find someone honest about their shortcomings or doubts of faith. There seemed to be more pretending than authenticity.

Faith-Filled Believers

I encountered a few people who I perceived had vibrant relationships with God, and something was different about them. They seemed to have an intimacy with Him and spoke in a different tone. Warmth and confidence shone in them, as if they knew God personally, like a friend. Their smiles were broader, and peace emanated from them.

My childhood primary church teacher, Miss Hanson, was one of those faith-filled believers. She invested in the first through third grade children of our church, and I was blessed to be one of them. We sang from children's hymnals Miss Hanson made for us, with colorful stickers placed around the handwritten lyrics for each song. She told us stories with flashcard pictures, opened her Bible, and taught us lessons about God that were not Bible stories. She taught us about God's character and His heart for us. We took turns being ushers for the offering collected in a plastic bank, shaped like a church building with a little slot in the roof for coins. She treated us as though we were important and worth investing in.

When Miss Hanson led us in singing, she radiated a joy that wooed my heart. She sang each word as though it were true and she believed it. Her stunning white hair, face, and smile drew me to the heart of Jesus. She knew Him. She trusted Him. I could tell. I wanted to stand near her in hopes that whatever she had with God could spill over onto me. She stood tall and confident and was the most beautiful woman I had ever seen.

Then there was Mr. Estabrook, my Awana commander. His daughter, my school friend, invited me to attend this children's Bible memory program at their church. Little did she know what an impact her father would have on my life. Mr. Estabrook married late in life, having been in the military as a young adult. He came to know Jesus after he had done some surly things in his youth. What those things were, we never knew, but when he talked to us kids, he spoke of Jesus and His love for us, always through many tears.

"You children, Jesus loves you. He loves you. He loves you very much. I know this because I was a merchant marine. I've done some terrible things in my life, and Jesus saved me. I tell you, He saved me. I can never repay Him for His great love for me. Never forget that, children. Jesus died for you on the cross because He loves you. Never forget how much He loves you."

He said the same thing week after week and I, indeed, have never forgotten it. His gratitude to Jesus was new to me. I had never seen anyone weep in thankfulness to Jesus like Mr. Estabrook did. I knew intuitively at the time that we should all be as grateful as he, but I didn't know how. To me, Jesus's death on the cross was a fact—an answer to spout in a Bible game or to quote in the context of a memory verse. Yes, I accepted Jesus as my Savior, and He lived in my heart, but it didn't mean much to me in my everyday life. I knew I would go to heaven when I died, but heaven felt a long time off. It didn't seem to help me then. I wanted to be like Mr. Estabrook. I wanted to have Jesus mean as much to me as He did to him.

Years later, as an adult, I wrestled with the reality of whether God was who He said He was. Yet, in my heart of hearts, I wanted to know Him like Miss Hanson and Mr. Estabrook did. How in the world could that happen when I was so bitter toward God?

A Door to Understanding

I scorned God because He didn't prevent my abuse. From my standpoint, if you love your child, you do whatever you can to keep them from harm. Protection means you stop abuse as it begins or, even better, you prevent it from ever happening.

I hated what I endured. I despised that incest colored my story. I wanted it not to be true. I wanted an escape route. In my finite mind, the only way to fix the pain of the abuse was for me to have been rescued from it. God is all-powerful. He could have stepped in and thwarted my father from ever touching me, and He didn't. How could dignity be restored in another way?

In my meetings with Rick, I continued to confess my disbelief in God's care for me. Rick was patient, never shaming me for my probing questions, which were laced with growing contempt.

"God doesn't love me! God doesn't care about me! How can you say that He does? If He loves me, He sure has a horrible way of showing it. I tell you He did absolutely nothing! He just sat there and watched as I was sexually abused. He did nothing!"

Rick sat for a second and then, with gentle firmness, responded. "Excuse me, Louise, but He did everything. He sent Jesus to die on the cross for every sin that was done to you. He did everything."

These words opened the door for me to a greater understanding of the gospel. I wanted to be rid of the sting of the shame and pain of the abuse by being rescued from it ever happening. Instead, Jesus rescued me through His death on the cross.

Privilege of Choice

God gives us all free will to choose. It is the way of love to get to choose. Without choice, love is not genuine. It is the same in any relationship. We choose whether we will receive love and respond in return. We decide if we want to follow God or go our own way. This gift of free will offers profound dignity. The creator of the universe gives us the privilege of choice.

I like the idea of having a choice, especially when I choose to do wrong. I want what I want when I want it, after all. In the moment of giving in to my sin, I welcome this plan of free will. I crave being selfish in my flesh. I don't, however, enjoy it so much when I feel the repercussions of someone else's free will, such as my father's free will or anyone who hurts me by their selfishness. I didn't take to the idea that I couldn't control my parents' free will. Because God loves my father, my mother, and others who harmed me, He gave them free will to choose His way or their way.

Our Representative and Substitute

If God were not a loving God, He would leave us to suffer through the consequences of sin without hope. Because He is love itself, He provided a way out of the suffering of sin and its effects. He didn't leave us in the aftermath of our own or others' free will. He sent Jesus, the innocent, sinless, and perfect Lamb of God, to take all our sin upon Himself so we wouldn't have to carry the sin or the shame of sin.

Jesus's death on the cross for our sins is the ultimate expression of love. When Jesus took the sin of my father's sexual abuse and the sin of my mother's passive neglect on the cross, Scripture says He actually became that sin, meaning He fully identified Himself with that sin: "God made him who had no sin to be sin for us, so that in him we might become the righteousness of God" (2 Cor. 5:21). My father's abuse was experienced by Jesus on the cross. He took that sin and felt the excruciating pain and shame of it. When my father abused me, he abused Jesus. When my mother stood idly by and watched the abuse happen, she hurt me, and she hurt the heart of Jesus.

It was not my parents' sin alone that Jesus carried on the cross. Jesus took my sinful independence on Himself, feeling the pain of it as He was crucified. My rage, my perfectionism, my arrogance, my critical spirit, my control—He took it all. When I sin in these ways because I want what I want when I want it, I remember it is my sin that crucified Him. In mercy and compassion for my brokenness, Jesus suffered for me. Isaiah 53:4–6 says, "Surely he took up our infirmities and carried our sorrows, yet we considered him stricken by God, smitten by him, and afflicted. But he was pierced for our transgressions, he was crushed for our iniquities; the punishment that brought us peace was upon him, and by his wounds we are healed. We all, like sheep, have gone astray, each of us has turned to his own way; and the Lord has laid on him the iniquity of us all."

In Nancy Stiehler Thurston's academic paper, "When Perfect Love Casts Out Fear," she said, "In his crucifixion, Jesus became the very embodiment of shame (e.g., his physical posture of extreme exposure and vulnerability on the cross; the crown of thorns with the mocking sign, 'This is the King of the Jews'). In the ultimate paradoxical gesture of divine love, Jesus became shame so that he might save us from the shame of separation from God. . . . The atonement of Jesus restored the interpersonal bridge between God and humans."[22] The solution for my sin and shame is Jesus.

A Beloved Child

God gave me the gift of free will so I would know that my response to Him is my own. I am not a pawn on His giant chess board. He gives me the freedom to receive Him or not. He stands with His arms extended to me, waiting for me to believe and receive this ultimate expression of love. When I think of being a parent and the joyful willing sacrifices I made out of love for my daughters, I have the smallest fraction of understanding of God's heart for me.

When Jesus bore my sorrows and suffering on the cross, He took my shame. He took upon Himself the consequences of what comes from my sin so I can experience healing and freedom. He took my shame and fear and carried it for me. He took my sin so my identity would no longer be what I did or what was done to me. He offered me an identity as a beloved child of God.

Grasping the Truth

With Rick's reminder that Christ did everything, the cross took on new meaning. God did not sit idly by on His throne when I was harmed, as I thought. Christ experienced the pain with me. He felt what I felt. He became that sin for me and paid the price for it, transferring it from my shoulders to His. He knew I needed a better solution than I could create for all the sin that harmed me—and for my shame. God knew I needed a Savior. He sent His only Son to become sin itself on the cross and allowed the effects of sin to destroy Him to death.

Fully grasping this truth brought me to tears. Jesus's death on the cross was no longer a historical fact or a ticket to a home in heaven. Understanding my need helped me to understand the power and beauty of the provision. It moved the understanding of His death from my head to my heart. Standing at the foot of the cross, knowing what I alone had done to crucify Jesus, made me worship. I was guilty, and He paid my debt. My tears of gratitude came because I knew I had done nothing to earn His substitutionary death. He took my sin and shame on the cross because of love. He is love itself and I, maybe for the first time in my life, began to grasp He loved me. He loved me. He *loves* me. He will always love me. Such love diminishes shame and produces worthiness. If I could live with this awareness all my days, I would die fulfilled and at peace.

It took time and more risking before I fully trusted God's love for me. As my confidence in His love grew, I found myself standing before loved ones, calling out with tears in my eyes, "Oh, friends, God loves us more than we can ever understand! I know this because He has forgiven me for so much. He paid for my sin and your sin. He paid for the sin that others have done to us. His love for us is so great. Never forget how much He loves you."

Chapter 11

SELF-PROTECTION TO GOD'S PROVISION

My personal life began to change. More growth was needed, but those closest to me discerned the difference. I wasn't as angry at God. I made more intentional choices to grasp the message of God's grace so I could mature in faith. I studied God's Word like it was my very breath. I saw the richness of it and wanted to eat it like food for my soul.

My understanding of the long-term process of healing grew. At first, I thought I could simply understand a truth, experience its benefits, and be fully healed. For example, when I understood my identity was not in what happened to me in my childhood, but in what was true about me as a child of God, I thought my struggle with the lie of my shame was done. I wanted my journey to be over, but the process of healing takes time, and there are lots of stops and starts. I learned that understanding truth was only the *first* step of healing in that area. Each time I was reminded of an old lie, I needed to practice believing truth instead. It was the process of learning to walk by the Spirit instead of by the flesh. Healing from shame is both a finished work of Jesus and an ongoing work of the Holy Spirit.

Shame is a manifestation of our flesh. Since we won't be free of our flesh until we enter heaven, shame will linger in us to varying degrees, depending on what we believe. When we forget who we are in Christ and who Jesus is, we will be susceptible to believing the lies that our shame tells us. Shame lifts as we walk in our new nature, believing our identity in Christ. "I have been crucified with Christ and I no longer live, but Christ lives in me. The life I live in the body, I live by faith in the Son of God, who loved me and gave himself for me" (Gal. 2:20). Believing His value in us lifts our shame. The more we believe it, the less shame we experience.

A key component of living by grace was to learn to trust the Holy Spirit as He helped me to risk believing truth. His role as our sanctifier—the one who matures us in Christ—is to give us power to believe and obey as we depend on Him. When I chose the efforts of my flesh, my fig leaves and my wall, I found I was stuck in my shame. The Holy Spirit was faithful to give me opportunities to practice believing and acting on each new truth about God and about me until I had a handle on it, freeing me to release the lies of my shame. It was and continues to be a slow but steady process.

Healing Steps

As I healed, I was trusted with small influence. I moved from being a participant in our 12-step support group to becoming one of the facilitators of it. I had a great deal of maturing yet to do, but I could share with others what God had taught me. As I did, I saw group members grow and begin to heal too. I was asked to share my story and what God had done in me for the worship service at church. I was humbled that God could and would use me after my long season of contempt toward Him. Since I learned and experienced the process of real forgiveness toward those who sinned against me, I tried to practice it in the smaller relational hurts I experienced. Forgiveness became authentic, and I understood it was the Holy Spirit within me who could do it.

The next step in my healing was to deal with the sin that the harm of the abuse ignited in me. My survival tools as a child—controlling behavior, rage, perfectionism, and arrogance—were no longer needed. I knew I should be gentle with myself for using them when I knew no other way to feel safe. It was appropriate to give myself grace. As a maturing adult, I no longer needed these protective measures to survive. It was time to learn to live in a healthy and constructive way for my family's and my sake. I needed to let go of the fig leaves that were a way of life for me.

The Battle

A battle ignited in my spirit. I wanted my parents to hold responsibility for my sinful self-protection. I believed I wouldn't have displayed such egregious behavior had I not been abused. Blaming and denial can feel right. It wasn't true. My self-protection was my responsibility alone. My control, arrogant superiority, perfectionism, and rage had been my companions and had given me the illusion of safety. I wasn't ready to give them up.

I didn't know how to live without my fig leaves. I knew the idol of these behaviors I held in my right hand was a lie (Isa. 44:20). They were an illusion. They kept me in control instead of depending on God. I wasn't ready to release them and hold onto Jesus's hand instead. I had been a Christian for thirty years and wasn't mature in faith. God knew and remained patient with me. He waited for me without condemnation of my process. He was gracious with me before I learned to be gracious with myself.

A year or so earlier, I learned I could only forgive if Jesus did the miracle of forgiveness in me. I was about to come to understand that I could only repent if Jesus did the work of repentance in me. It wasn't going to happen in me without His power. *But how?*

All through my life I had spoken words of repentance for various sins I committed, always with more fervor each time, as if really meaning it would give me the strength needed to get that sin under control. Yet the sin itself was the control. *How could I control my sin of control?*

Trying Harder

In my youth I was taught that repentance is making a spiritual U-turn. I shared this definition many times saying, "We are going one direction *toward* our sin, and we need to turn and run the opposite direction *away* from our sin." In this view of repentance, the effort for change is mine alone, and the success or failure of the reform rests on my shoulders. What's implied in the teaching is that if my commitment to Jesus is sincere, I must try harder to stop sinning. Repentance was taught without regard to the reality that we will sin again after we declare our desire to reform. This omission created confusion and shame in me.

I reflected on my years of carrying the little spiral notebook in my purse with all the verses on anger. I recited the words, "God, I repent of my rage," more times than I could count and yet the rage continued. "God, I must not have meant it last time I said it, but this time I know I do. Or at least I think I know I do. I will try harder to stop raging." When the rage didn't stop, I felt like a failure as a Christian. What was wrong with me?

A Greater Power

What I didn't understand was that repentance by my own will-power is unattainable because sin is stronger than I am. Repentance needs a power greater than me. It needs Jesus. Only Jesus can break the power of the sin and give me a new way to respond when I feel shame. First Peter 2:6 says, "The one who trusts in him will never be put to shame."

When Jesus died on the cross, He became sin for us. He took the penalty for our sin and bore our sorrows. When He rose from the dead, He broke the power of sin and death by showing He was greater than both. Because I trusted Jesus and His work for me, His resurrection power dwells within me by the Holy Spirit. He *in me* is able to overcome my sin. He can do the work of repentance in me.

The Greek word for *repentance* means "a turning." It's a pivot from my desire to cover my shame in my own strength and turning to the only one who has the power to defeat my sin. Repentance in practice is me approaching God in prayer: "Holy Spirit, I continue to sin by taking matters into my own hands, trying to meet my needs in my way. I hurt You, myself, and others in the process. I can't stop unless You help me. In fact, I can't even *want* to stop unless You do that work for me. Spirit of God, will You deal with this sin in me? Will You do the work of repentance in me?"

Fear of Letting Go

When I first understood these powerful promises that Christ in me is stronger than my sin, I was full of hope and gladly turned over my sin of perfectionism. It felt like boulders were taken off my shoulders. The out-of-control anger was another story. I feared letting it go. How would my needs be met if I didn't demand it? My lack of desire to repent of my rage revealed I did not yet trust God to meet my personal need to be valued, respected, and loved.

In *Behind the Mask*, Bill Thrall, Bruce McNicol, and John Lynch described the struggle with anger like this: "When we have been hurt or have hurt another, a deep need to be validated grows within us. We must hold onto our 'rightness' at all costs, and so we strive to control every area in our life. Control validates our rightness and soothes our anger. If we give up any form of control to another, we have somehow proven we must not be right and our anger will emerge."[23] Anger made me feel in control. Anger made me feel right. I needed a reform that was authentic, effective, and produced safety for my heart. My self-protective rage was only ever an illusion of met needs.

First, I had to admit what was true. I trusted my rage more than I trusted God—and I didn't want to stop. I didn't believe God would show up. For perfectionism, that seemed possible, but not the rage. That was too big. My needs to feel safe, valued, and respected were legitimate. The only way I knew to guarantee these valid needs would be met was if I demanded through rage. I had no idea how to let God meet those needs in me. I didn't yet trust God to care for me. I didn't know how to wait for the provision to be met. I had only ever depended on myself through my rage, wall, and other fig leaves.

After I learned about repentance and what was true about the power of the Holy Spirit in me, Rick encouraged me to repent of my rage. My bold response was to tell him that I didn't want to. I was in denial of how serious my rage issues were, which seems silly in retrospect because of my shame for it, but the denial remained. I felt entitled to hang on to it. I didn't know what to do.

Facing the Damage

Rick encouraged me to go home and talk with my family. It was critical for me to understand how my rage affected others. Up until that point I was blind to it. I liked the sense of control and safety I felt when I exploded. He told me to ask for a family meeting. I was to ask my daughters and husband to share with me how my anger affected them. Anticipation of this meeting began to bring me out of denial. I felt anxious.

Desire for freedom from the bondage-producing behavior over-came my fear, and I gathered everyone together. Rachel was three years old, and Emily was seven. I sat in the middle of our couch with the girls on either side of me and Chuck close at hand.

I began, "We all know Mommy has a problem with anger. I need your help. The next time I'm angry, please tell me how my anger is affecting you."

Rachel looked straight at me and said, "Oh, no, Mommy. I won't do that. You are too scary when you are angry."

I turned to my sweet Emily and, though she said nothing, tears ran down her face. I then glanced at Chuck, and he uttered not a word. The pained expression on his face as he cast his eyes toward the ground said it all.

The denial evaporated, and I began to face the ugliness of my sin and the relational destruction it created. The wounds I caused my family by my out-of-control anger ran deep. They had every right to not trust me. In that instant I became willing to repent of my rage. My family helped me to be honest with myself about the damage of it. They helped me face my guilt. Embracing my responsibility for the sin and the destruction of it freed me to healthy shame. It gave me an opportunity to stand once again in front of the cross, confessing my need for a Savior.

I came before God and poured out my heart to Him. "God, I have harmed my family more than I can comprehend. I confess my sin of rage to You. Thank You for Your forgiveness. I want to live another way. Holy Spirit, I can't stop unless You help me to stop. Thank You, Jesus, for dying on the cross for my sin and the destruction that my sin has caused. Thank You for conquering sin and death by rising from the dead. Thank You that You are stronger than my rage. Oh, God, I repent of my rage. Spirit of God, will You do the work of repentance in me?"

The miracle began.

Resurrection Power

Dependency on the indwelling Holy Spirit fuels repentance. After that first day of repentance, if I opened my heart and hands to Him,

He showed up to free me to calm down and be at rest instead of giving into my anger. When I wanted to rage, I turned to Him and said, "Holy Spirit, I want to rage right now. I can't stop in my own strength. Let the resurrection power of Christ help me to trust You and obey rather than give in to what my flesh is screaming to do." Each time I humbled my heart in this way, I felt encouraged by the change in me.

Repentance, like forgiveness, is a process. I would like to report that I never raged again, but it wouldn't be true. At times I didn't want to trust and obey. Even though I had the Holy Spirit in me and could choose surrender and obedience, I sometimes gave into my flesh, giving myself permission to rail at someone. Repentance doesn't mean we won't ever sin again. It means we trust God to do the work in us as we choose to allow Him to do it. The more I trusted God with my fear, shame, and sin, the less I raged. It was not my effort to stop raging that slowed my raging. The power that raised Jesus from the dead accomplished it and is still accomplishing the work of repentance in me by the Holy Spirit. The Holy Spirit in me is greater than my rage, perfectionism, blaming, desire to gossip, or whatever self-reliant fig leaf I want to use to meet my needs for value and love apart from God and others.

Admitting I didn't want to stop raging was an important step of the process. If I had pretended to be willing to repent before I was ready, nothing would have changed. In telling the truth, I brought what was in darkness into the light. The light is where healing occurs (John 3:19). As long as I kept the permission I gave myself to rage hidden, it held power in me. Through confession, the repentance process began in me.

Repentance is a gift from God. It is a gift to heal our shame and free us to live in the dignity He created in us. The shame for my rage, arrogant superiority, blaming, people pleasing, perfectionism, and overeating can be healed through repentance. As the Holy Spirit does the work of repentance in us, we can live out of our dignity and who we are in Christ.

We are no longer defined by our besetting sins and shame. We are defined by Him. We carry a noble identity as adopted sons and daughters of the King of Kings.

The more I trusted God to do the work of repentance in me, the less I sinned. I carried less shame because my guilt lifted. I could love more. It was encouraging to walk into a room and not think of sizing up people to decide if I was more or less important than they were. I began to walk into a room of people and delight in who was there, whether I already knew them or was about to meet them for the first time. To walk into a room of people and not be self-focused felt like victory. Because it was. And the victory belonged to Jesus.

Chapter 12

CONTROL TO FREEDOM

I am, by God's design, a truth teller. I am passionate about it. My motive may be the fallout from growing up in a home that exhibited hiddenness and pretending as a lifestyle. It is also a gift the Holy Spirit gave me when I came to know Jesus. Truth is what sets a person free (John 8:32), and I want freedom. I want it for me and everyone I meet. Sometimes I like truth and other times I don't. But when I wrestle with truth, I know I will experience freedom when I submit to it. Our country was founded on the premise of freedom and the desire of every human being to enjoy it. We can fear freedom if we don't understand the beauty of it. Imprisonment is strangely comforting when it is all you know. The recidivism rate of our penal system should tell us something about that. If you don't know what freedom looks or feels like, it can be confusing and even frightening. If you don't know how to live in it, it can seem elusive, even when it is in your grasp.

The Twelve-Inch Gap

Nancy saw the imprisonment I was in early on. She quoted Galatians 5:1 to me often and asked me to memorize it: "It is for freedom that Christ has set us free. Stand firm, then, and do not let yourselves be burdened again by a yoke of slavery." Because Nancy lived in freedom, she kept wooing me to it and step by step helped me to live in it. Nancy knew I needed to be set free and that the 12-step program could be used by God to liberate me.

My critical judgment of the 12 Steps of A.A. in my younger years revealed I didn't understand the truth or wisdom of them. I didn't like the phraseology in step 2 of "a power greater than ourselves," or in step 3, "God as we understand Him." Without a clear understanding of what is meant by these steps, I believed the writers of these steps, Bill W and Dr. Bob, were universalists. I assumed they taught and promoted that members could design a god they wanted and then ask for his or her help. I judged the motive of their words to be foolish. I could not have been more wrong.

The reality is everyone submits to God as much as they *truly* believe and trust. If I can spout elaborate theology but don't believe it for myself, that theology is meaningless to my everyday experience with God. Bill W and Dr. Bob knew this from their own lives and in working with other alcoholics. Though I know truth about God, if I don't have an intimate walk with Him, I won't open my heart to Him or bow my knee before Him. I won't experience Him relationally as a friend.

In the beginning of my journey of healing, I had a twelve-inch gap between my head and my heart. I attended Bible college. I knew the tenets of Scripture. I memorized hundreds of verses in my childhood alone. I could lead Bible studies through challenging doctrinal passages and teach the attributes of God in my sleep. I could give the soteriological accomplishments of Jesus at the cross and resurrection, explain the five points of Calvinism and debate which ones I held to, discuss dispensationalism, and teach through the types of Christ in the Old Testament. Yet I lived in utter shame, believing God was not who He claimed to be and I was not loved by Him as His Word promised. Shame had its way in me, and I didn't know what to do about it.

It has been said that the whole of the Christian life is a journey to trust God. I believe this is true. Even if I know a great deal *about* God, it takes a lifetime to learn to trust Him fully. At some point we decide whether we will humble ourselves before a holy God. We determine if we will learn to trust Him with ourselves.

The First Step

In the first of the 12 Steps, we admit we are powerless over something in our lives we cannot control: alcohol, drugs, rage, lust, pride, people pleasing, codependency, or whatever counterfeit we use to run from God and ourselves. Coming to the awareness of powerlessness over the messy reality of our lives softens our hearts and helps us realize we're not in control as we'd like to believe. It brings us to an understanding of healthy shame, which reminds us we are not superior or inferior to others. We are on level ground in front of the cross, all in need of a Savior.

As we read through the steps in our Adult Children of Alcoholics meetings, I found I could identify with the first one. It says: "We admitted we were powerless over the effects of family dysfunction, that our lives had become unmanageable."[24] I had been striving to do everything right, even after attending a church founded on God's grace. I made a mess of my marriage, my family, and my own life by my driven perfectionism and rage. My life was unmanageable. The control I craved slipped through my fingers, and I began to understand that I never held it in the first place.

The black-and-white approach to life my father instilled in me felt safe. Tell me what is right and wrong, and I'll follow the rules and know what to do. In this approach, everything has a place, a sense of order and control. I understood the lure of it. Everything is about absolutes. All perspectives—opinions, convictions, preferences, passions, and theology—are sorted into black-and-white categories. One is right; the other is wrong. It seemed like an ideal approach to life since I didn't know how to think for myself. Then I lived a little and discovered that sometimes there are two rights and two wrongs in opposing opinions. And there is a lot of gray.

I knew with God there are absolute truths: Jesus is the Son of God. The Bible is the inspired Word of God. God is the highest rule and authority. Jesus died for the sin of the world. He rose again to conquer sin and death. All absolute truths. I could lean on these foundations and rest, but much of the "truth" I was taught early on wasn't absolute. It was my father's or someone else's opinions, convictions, and perhaps mere clever ideas. And sometimes what I learned as absolute truth was plain wrong.

Nowhere in Scripture does it say anything about women shaving their legs. Nowhere in Scripture does it say Christians don't drink or dance. Nowhere in Scripture does it say Christians are going to be punished for their sin. Disciplined? Yes. Punished? No. Big difference.

Living in the Gray

I had a formidable learning curve to undo the wrong and incomplete teaching I received for decades. The process included learning to live with gray and multiple opinions. I didn't know there was more than one delicious recipe for chocolate chip cookies. More than one way to properly make a bed, park a car, wash a dish, shake someone's hand, spend money, exercise, or even vote. The moment I met someone who deeply loved Jesus and identified with a different political party than me, I was undone. It was a good education for me.

This education included relational conflicts. Within my marriage, I believed if I was hurt, Chuck had to be wrong. He wore the black hat, and I wore the white. No matter that Chuck implored the pure motive of his heart, if I was hurt, I was wronged. My pain meant I was innocent and

Chuck was guilty. In my hurt, I read his motive as selfish and uncaring. Why else would a husband not buy thoughtful birthday presents for a wife except that he was self-consumed? It couldn't be that his own father never once bought a present for his mother, thus Chuck hadn't learned the skill of gift giving. I was sure my evaluation of Chuck's motive was correct, that he didn't care. Nine times out of ten I was convinced his motive was not love for me, but love for self. I'm certain he felt defeated in his efforts to be tender toward me since I didn't recognize it.

My veils of shame gave me a distorted view of him and his behaviors. In *Facing Shame*, authors Merle A. Fossum and Marilyn J. Mason said, "[Shame] is a cancer that grows from feeling bad about oneself to interpreting neutral or impersonal experiences in personally deprecating ways."[25] As I became willing to let go of control, I understood that many of my hurts from Chuck were unintentional. His efforts were evidence of the sincerity of his love for me. In time I began to appreciate his choices to risk buying anything for me. His gifts demonstrated his selflessness, especially after I criticized him for failing to give me a present I liked.

Black-and-White World

My understanding of life, thank you, God, turned upside down. I learned that desiring a black-and-white world meant I wanted the world under my control—an unreachable goal. I can't make the world what I want it to be. Until I understood this, I believed when someone disagreed with me or did something in a different way, they were wrong. They were not behaving as Jesus would. How convenient. The problem isn't me and my need for control. The problem is the other person, the other group, or the other culture. In this black-and-white system, I never have to learn to love someone unlike me, and I don't have to learn to trust anyone but myself. If others are doing something I believe they shouldn't do, I can distance myself from them all in the name of righteous living. I justified this by quoting John 2:24–25: "But Jesus would not entrust himself to them, for he knew all men. He did not need man's testimony about man, for he knew what was in a man."

In a black-and-white life management system, I am crippled by living as a victim. When I think black and those around me think white, I feel dismissed or overlooked. "Shame often prompts us to view ourselves as victims. Consequently, whether we blame others or condemn ourselves for our actions, we sink into the depths of feeling sorry for ourselves," explained Harriet Lerner in *The Dance of Fear*.[26] I don't like to admit this because of how powerless it feels to be a victim. When I judge I have been victimized, I prefer the feeling of believing I'm innocent in how I respond to life and to people. If I'm innocent, I don't have to change. I can blame others for what they've done wrong. If they don't change what they are doing to suit me, then I remain in the power position of being the judge. I can feel justified in withholding acceptance of them so I feel safe and powerful. In that posture I am not the victim. I am the one who is right. If I am hurt, then I am right and I give myself permission to hurt in return for the hurt done to me.

Shame produced a victim mentality in me—as though I expected to be disregarded and overlooked. I couldn't discern it that way at the time. When I was hurt, I received it as a confirmation of what I believed to be true about me. Of course I wouldn't be invited to the party. Of course I would have a job where my boss took advantage of me. Of course it would be my line at the grocery store or the bank that was the slowest. Of course. The problem was me. I didn't want this to be true, so I blamed and poured contempt on others for how they made me feel. I believed if they were wearing the black hat, then I wore the white one, the one acceptable and worthy to be respected and loved.

Until I could learn to let go of control and let go of having to wear the white hat and not the black hat, until I could rest in the places of life that were gray, I would live in shame and fear. I wouldn't be free. I could never let go of control until I learned to trust someone besides myself. I could never let go of control until I saw it for the illusion it is.

Control provides a false sense of security. It tricks us into believing we are the ones who have caused our world to be as we want it. We are not that powerful. We may demand that others respond to us as we wish, but we cannot command their hearts. They may be compliant on the outside but full of resentment on the inside. Attempts to direct our circumstances to reflect our ideal will at some point run into roadblocks beyond our ability to overcome.

Seeing the Right Motive

Believe it or not, my criticism of Chuck didn't motivate him to try to discover what I might enjoy as a gift. My demand that he try harder and give it a little more thought didn't give him courage to risk loving me. He felt controlled and criticized. His heart didn't feel safe with me. My attempts to control Chuck backfired. They didn't produce the result of my needs being met through experiencing his love. He couldn't love me from the heart when he felt controlled.

When I understood that my husband didn't intentionally hurt me when his gifts missed my heart, I could allow him to be a human being on his own journey to be the great husband he wanted to be. I could then see his thoughtful and honoring true motive. I could receive the gift of his love and let it fill my heart even if I didn't care for the actual gift he purchased. It wasn't about him hitting a bullseye in his gift giving. It was about me recognizing his courageous effort and receiving his heartfelt choices to care for me. It took me out of the victim's posture and out of the role of the judge. It allowed me to give grace to him as another person learning to love. He was more like me than I realized and maybe, just maybe, I could learn to trust him if I would see his motive as being for me instead of against me.

It was the same with people in authority. When decisions were made by bosses or leaders that produced adverse effects, I assumed their motive was a negative one. I wasn't interested in hearing their reasoning and believed the worst about them. As I became willing to see their point of view, I began to understand that sometimes hard decisions must be made that bring painful consequences for everyone or for some. It is one of the challenges of leadership. When unfortunate decisions are made by leaders who lack integrity or good judgment, we can learn to rely on God, knowing He is greater than the consequences of those decisions. He will care for us in how those decisions land on us. And we can employ our voices to stand up for ourselves in respectful ways.

Firm Foundation

Learning to live in the gray helped me learn to trust. Staying in a black-and-white perception of life kept me afraid, judgmental, and full of shame. The process of letting go of rigid thinking helped me emerge from denial that I could make life what I wanted it to be. It freed me. I learned that even if circumstances and relationships weren't my ideal, I would remain in God's hands. I can choose to hold onto my shame and fear, or I can learn to trust someone greater than myself who is in control of everything. The firm foundation under my feet will hold me fast, and I can trust Him. He is my rock and fortress.

Shame has a grip on us in a black-and-white world because we don't have to trust. In that world we remain in control, and control never brings freedom. The illusion of control is a counterfeit of what our hearts long for. We assume control will bring safety, but instead it brings bondage. Real control lies in the hands of our Sovereign God. We are unable to hold all things in our hands as He does.

As we learn to let go, as we learn to trust, we can begin to lean into the One who is the truth, and in Him we find rest. We can stand in Him, gaining a firm footing, and release our control to Him, experiencing His love for us in every detail of our lives. This is where the freedom lies—in trusting Him. When I am free, I can trust, I can love, I can live without the hindrance of my fear. In freedom I can be loved and known without a wall or a veil of shame to cloud my vision. *This* is healing.

Chapter 13

SCARCITY TO GRATITUDE

In our early years in Phoenix, money was scarce. Chuck and I worked hard at jobs that were anything but lucrative. I love children and I love teaching, but preschools aren't institutions where good work ethic, passion, and skill produce a decent salary. Chuck's vocation as a church musician was no different. We were often behind in our bills. It was a challenge to break even.

In our Christian circles, mothers stayed home to raise their children while husbands carried the sole responsibility as providers. Women often criticized me for working outside the home. They told me whatever money a woman makes is extra, and a family should learn to live on the husband's salary alone. That seemed easy for them because their husbands made adequate incomes. The sacrifices made for the wife to stay home were minimal. Not so with us. I worked to pay for our utilities and buy food. Chuck's salary covered our rent. We had no health insurance or vacation money. We washed cloth diapers for our babies and hung them on the clothesline to dry. Chuck rode the bus to and from work and school. Opportunities for our children to participate in sports or extracurricular activities were nonexistent. We lived frugally and made it work.

Looking back, I am proud of us for doing as well as we did within our income. Our girls never knew we struggled financially. My oldest daughter, Emily, was given beautiful hand-me-down clothes by generous friends. I didn't have to shop for her until she was ten years old. God was faithful to us.

At the time I couldn't see God's provision through the veils of my shame. The message I received from our tight budget was that we were unworthy of abundance. We Americans live better than most of the world, but it didn't mean much to me. I compared with neighbors and noticed the differences between us. I interpreted our financial status as confirmation from God that we would perpetually be in want. I feared we would continue to lack—because I didn't deserve more.

Relational Needs

My fear of ongoing want was not limited to material needs. It included my fears regarding relational needs. I feared that my valid needs for respect, love, security, attention, belonging, and value would not be recognized or honored, creating more scars in my heart.

When we fear scarcity of any kind of needs, it is often because we have a history of neglect, whether perceived or real. We assume God and others will respond to us with that same disregard.

Since my parents abused and then walked away from me, I anticipated disinterest or rejection from those I loved and admired. I believed it was up to me to meet my own needs. I presumed no one would choose to be a friend because they liked me.

Avoiding an Empty Bucket

What flows from a heart filled with shame is a sense of not enough. We each carry an imaginary bucket, scrambling for someone to fill it so we can believe we are enough. We blame ourselves, God, or others for the lack.

I evaluate myself and find faults that explain others' disinterest in me. If I were better at a skill valued in my circles, I'd feel confident, and my bucket would be full. If I were more intelligent, more attractive, more humorous, more successful, stronger and more capable, I would feel filled up. If I could be the one chosen at work, if I could have a new car, if I could send my kids to a private college, if, if, if. I believe I wouldn't feel as I do if my life were orchestrated in the right way.

When we do this, we expect that pleasure or admiration from others will give us what we need. But many wealthy, beautiful, intelligent, and successful people are unhappy. What fills our bucket cannot be a perfect life or a life that turns out as we wish. Nothing we try to do will remove the shame that created the empty bucket in the first place.

For many of us, it can be distasteful or downright scary to admit we have needs. Admitting our legitimate relational needs can make us feel weak. Neediness implies weakness—and no one wants that. Refusal to acknowledge our needs may seem like a good strategy to avoid appearing inadequate, but it isn't effective. Instead, it increases our fragility because of the wall it builds around our hearts. We were never meant to meet our own needs.

If we believe we can be self-sufficient, people can sense otherwise. We may not have a conscious awareness of our neediness, but those around us feel it because of our direct or indirect reminders of how they fail us. Whether we recognize it or not, our demand for our relational needs to be met and our belief that others continually disappoint us reveals what we believe. What they do is not enough to make us feel filled up. When we believe the lie of our shame, we are not enough and whatever others do cannot satisfy.

Blaming Others or Self

I can feel hurt and resentment when friends and loved ones don't come through for me as I wish. Sometimes I'd like them to read my mind and know what I desire. When I anticipated someone's attention to my needs and it didn't happen, I stood in condemnation of them. I perceived their actions as neglectful. I blamed them for the emptiness I felt. I thought if they loved and cared for me, they should nurture me in the way I wanted.

Marriages dissolve over this struggle.

People leave churches because they don't feel pursued.

Employees resign from their jobs because they don't feel valued.

If I have no expectations of a person, employer, or church to meet my relational needs, I don't become inflamed when they make mistakes or seem selfish. If, however, I have an unspoken agenda for someone to meet my needs in a certain way and they don't, I assign motive to them of their perceived rejection, even though I may use other words:

"This church is full of cliques."

"He only ever thinks of himself."

"This company doesn't value older employees."

"That teacher plays favorites."

"I knew my friend wouldn't follow through on calling me. She's a phony."

I do this because I fear that the friend, church, company, or teacher discovered what I tried to keep hidden. I am not enough. I walk away with the lie of my shame confirmed. Then I point at my perceived offender so everyone looks at them instead of at me and the emptiness I see in my bucket.

Other times we can excuse inappropriate behavior of those we love, taking the blame when the fault is not ours. A man may believe he caused his wife's affair, but this is not true. Mistakes do not justify the breaking of marriage vows. It can seem more palatable to bear the responsibility for someone else's harm of us than to face our loved one's selfishness or insensitivity. In shame, we don't know what is tolerable. We are used to being overlooked.

Two Lies

Looking for people to fill us up never works long term. Trying to make the world as we want it to be is impossible. The roller coaster of pleasant and unpleasant experiences in life cannot be controlled. Happy circumstances and people responding to us as we wish cannot heal shame. Without healing the wound that fuels our shame messages, shame will continue to rear its ugly head when life and relationships don't go our way.

Two lies work together when we believe our needs are unmet because of our flaws. The first lie is our inferiority. We know this is false because everyone is equally valued by God. "God so loved the world" (John 3:16), and that means all of us. There are no greater or lesser people. The second lie is that our needs are unmet. The truth is that God has supplied *all* our needs, not only our physical needs. Our spiritual, emotional, and relational needs are included.

> His divine power has given us everything we need for life
> and godliness through our knowledge of him who called us
> by his own glory and goodness. (2 Pet. 1:3)
> The Lord is my shepherd, I shall not be in want. (Ps. 23:1)

And my God will meet all your needs according to his
glorious riches in Christ Jesus. (Phil. 4:19)

These verses are not the proverbial carrot on a string in front of
our noses to trick us into believing what may never happen. They are
the promises of God, and He must and will carry them through. He
will be true to who He has declared Himself to be. He is Jehovah Jireh,
God Who Provides. He is the Good Shepherd and the guardian of our
souls. When I have a sense of scarcity, it is because I have my eyes in the
wrong place.

Always Full

God's Word declares that my needs are already met in Christ. In
fact, my bucket is never empty but always full. Trusting this truth gives
me the opportunity to shift my focus to the One who looks on me with
delight and deep value. When I am ready to repent and let go of my
agenda and expectation for how my needs will be met, God lifts the veils
of my shame so I can witness the abundance that has been in my life all
along. A full bucket proves that my shameful perception of myself is a lie.

I had a hard time recognizing this at first. All I could see was what
I didn't have. In my interpretation there was no bounty. In my shame I
didn't know how to recognize this provision, so I asked God to give me
eyes to see Him. I invited Him to open my eyes to the gifts of His love
every day. I asked Him to do the work of repentance in me that would
free me to release my controlling agenda of how my needs should be met.

Repentance began with learning to be thankful for what I had. I
began a practice of daily recording ten gifts that proved God's love and
care for me. I needed to discover He met my needs when others didn't.
At first it took me a good thirty minutes at day's end to recall ten gifts
from God. Now it takes less than five minutes to recognize God's gifts
to me from the previous twenty-four hours. God has cultivated in me a

grateful heart. This gratitude has changed how I see my life and how I see my bucket.

My list can include things like a good night's sleep, laughter with friends, kindness from a child, the privilege of praying with a hurting brother or sister in Christ, being used by God to encourage another, hearing thunder and seeing lightning in a summer monsoon storm, hot running water in the shower, spectacles for my aging eyes, a Scripture that reveals God's character to me, a hug from a preschooler, support from a coworker. The more I recounted, the more humble my heart became. I recognized the lavish love He poured on me like a cherished child. I wasn't just tolerated. He delighted in me. Instead of feeling scarcity, I found myself regularly weeping as I recognized His intentional love for me. For *me*. Not for the whole world, but for me personally.

An Overflowing Bucket

Beyond the daily gestures of affection God gives me, the greatest expression of His love for me was in sending His Son to die for me, freeing me from the destruction of sin and giving me new life in Him. When my bucket seems empty, I know I have lost connection with what He has done for me. Shame creates a veil over my eyes and prevents me from seeing it. When all else is a broken mess in my life and God's goodness seems remote, I must think of what He has done for me through Jesus. I remember His sacrificial love, and the shame lifts. Singing a hymn or praise song gives me words for the blessings I can forget in my shame.

What flows from a heart healing from shame is gratitude and trust. When I am grateful, it reminds me of how God values me. The personal gifts He gives me each day and the gift of my new life in Christ humble me and free me to trust Him. Shame and gratitude cannot coexist. When I receive God's abundance, I rest in His presence, content with my life and what I have because of what is true about me and about

Him. The burden of my shame lifts and is replaced with a light but full bucket. I can run wherever He leads me.

From this soul-filled trust we can join with the prophet Habakkuk to declare the goodness and provision of God: "Though the fig tree does not bud and there are no grapes on the vines, though the olive crop fails and the fields produce no food, though there are no sheep in the pen and no cattle in the stalls, yet I will rejoice in the Lord, I will be joyful in God my Savior. The Sovereign Lord is my strength; he makes my feet like the feet of a deer, he enables me to go on the heights" (Hab. 3:17–19). He is enough. His provision, power, and love fill my bucket to overflowing.

Chapter 14
COMPARISON TO CONTENTMENT

Life was a competition that made me tired. I learned early on to place everyone, including myself, on a rating scale, hoping to find others less able than me so I could lessen the exposure of my deficiencies. Where did I rank? If I was at the top of the scale, I was safe. If I was at the bottom of the scale, I was unsafe. Shame drove the rating scale. Because I was shame based, the rating was relentless.

My bondage to comparison started in grade school. I excelled in academics, always in the top reading and math groups. Thanks to piano lessons from my mother and a God-given natural ability, I was ahead of the curve for choir and band. On the other hand, I couldn't hit a softball with a bat to save my life. My art projects had glue dripping down the sides. I recall the sting of being one of the last chosen for teams in gym class, and the high I felt standing at the blackboard in math competitions when I often got the answer first.

Because of my shame, I compare. And when I compare, it increases my shame. Harriet Lerner, in her book *The Dance of Fear*, said, "Comparisons breed shame."[27]

Replica of Pompeii

Since healing from destructive shame is a gradual one, the consequence of my struggle with comparison affected my daughters. I saw my children as an extension of myself. I didn't know how to let my kids be people in process. I don't think I am alone in this struggle. I've seen it in other parents who want their children to be superior to others so they will be valued and admired. When they are, we, as parents, are then valued and admired.

This parental competition displayed itself one year when Emily, our oldest daughter, was in fourth grade. The students were to create a model of an ancient city—a replica—not a report about it. I felt uneasy. Unlike me, Emily is a gifted athlete. Like me, Emily is not artistically inclined. We were in trouble. The instructions said parents could help, but the majority was to be the student's work. The due date was the day before Open House night so the models would be on display for all to see. I gulped.

Emily chose the city of Pompeii. We went to the library to do research. She took notes, and we created a plan. We found items around the house to transform into replicas of buildings, homes, and details of the ancient city. We had fun crafting the model together on our living room floor. Then Emily lost interest in the project.

Elements were missing to do the model justice, so I cajoled Emily, reminding her that everyone would see it. She was fine with it as it was and would have been satisfied with a grade of B or C. I, however, was not. I wanted her project to be a standout, or at least something that wasn't going to make me feel embarrassed. The model had become a reflection of *me*. I found myself pacing around the unfinished replica of Pompeii on the living room floor, trying to justify in my mind what I was about to do.

And then I did it. I began to finish the project without her. I eased my conscience by calling Emily into the room to glue, paint, hold something in place, or suggest where a building should be positioned. I did what the teacher told the parents not to do. I did what Emily should have and could have done. I completed the model myself. Though she did most of the work, I did more than I should have. I did it because of my pride and my shame.

Open House Night

On Open House night, we found "her" project in the middle of the classroom near the other models. I felt guilt and shame for my actions, yet thankful that Pompeii held its own. As I looked closer at the other replicas, it seemed other parents struggled too. Some cities looked like an architect had built them. The precise lines and intricate details took a deft hand to maneuver. Then there was Pompeii, a little rougher, but still beyond the scope of a ten-year-old girl. I was glad I was not alone in my guilt, but it didn't make me feel better.

What intrigued me most were two models of cities set off to the side, away from the center. Perhaps the most honest projects, these were the handiwork of children. They were crude models made with play-dough, displaying the handwriting of a ten-year-old on the label. The integrity of these parents revealed my pride and the fear in my shame. I wished for the personal confidence and strength to be like those parents.

I wanted to be different. I didn't want shame to hold the power in my life that it did. I didn't want comparison or the shame behind it to drive me to dishonor my child, the teacher, or myself. Still, it did. How could I live in a new way when I didn't know any other?

Measuring Up

If you asked me that Open House night, I would have told you that all of us are valuable, and each of us has differing strengths and weaknesses. No one is good at everything. But when one is shame based, it is important to be viewed in your strengths. Though I knew I had strengths, for me, they didn't balance out the enormity of my perceived weaknesses.

Shame tells us we don't have what it takes. We will not be valued, admired, or embraced as we are. If we could be as talented, attractive, intelligent, popular, clever, or successful as those we compare ourselves to, we wouldn't feel shame. The dilemma is that there will always be someone with more ability than we have. To be honest about our strengths and weaknesses and find contentment and confidence with our station in life is a work of God in us. When I am content and confident in who I am and with my life circumstances, the need to compare and the shame that fuels the comparison diminishes.

If our ability to be confident and content lies solely in what we can achieve, we will become driven to perform well in our strengths and hide our weaknesses. We will push those we love to do the same. And what if the ones we love can't be pushed because they don't share our same drivenness or strengths? They won't feel accepted for who they are. They won't feel safe with us.

When my desire to have Pompeii look like something more than Emily could create as a fourth grader, the project became about my pride and shame instead of her education. Because I wanted her to perform well for my sake, I hindered her from experiencing the natural consequences that would have come from an unfinished project for school. I wanted her to look good, and in turn, for me to look good, when Pompeii was on display on Open House night.

My lack of confidence in myself and in God's work in Emily were evident. Greater still was the realization that I felt the need to compete with others for love and acceptance. This competition fuels comparison. My shame told me I needed to show superiority or at least hit par for me to be respected. It was up to me.

Risk Believing the Truth

Freedom from shame cannot come from achievement or notoriety. It comes when I know I am accepted as I am, when I know I am valued and loved in my imperfect humanity. Freedom from shame happens when I receive and experience love. Only then can comparisons diminish. When I know I am loved and accepted, competition is no longer needed. I no longer need to pretend to be my ideal self—in an attempt to hide my shame self. I can be my real self.

Like repentance and forgiveness, learning to receive love is a process. Since I had not been loved well as a child, I would need to learn to receive love by faith. I needed to risk believing the truth of God's love before I could fall back on an experience of it, otherwise I would remain stuck.

The truth of God's love for me moved from my head to my heart when I understood the gift of Jesus's death on the cross. That shift produced a new freedom and healing, but I had not yet learned how to receive God's love in the routine moments of life. As I practiced gratitude, I grew in awareness of His love for me. Step by step, God removed more veils of my shame so I might experience His affection in my heart. But I didn't know how to connect with it. I felt clumsy and awkward. Was I to sit in a chair and wait for it to fall on me? That seemed weird. I knew I needed to recognize and experience it, but I felt blind and numb.

I decided I would ask God to reveal His love to me in my experience. "Show me, God," I said. "Show me Your love. Your Word tells me You love me with an unfailing and everlasting love, but I don't know how to experience it. I want to *feel* your love. I have no idea how to do it. Help me know how to receive your love."

I looked up verses on God's love:
God is love. (1 John 4:8)
The Lord your God is with you,

he is mighty to save.
He will take great delight in you,
 he will quiet you with his love,
 he will rejoice over you with singing. (Zeph. 3:17).
Let them give thanks to the Lord for his unfailing love
 and his wonderful deeds for men. (Ps. 107:15)

I wrote these and other verses on pieces of paper and posted them around my house. I taped them on the window over my kitchen sink, on my refrigerator, on my bathroom mirror and the mirror over my dresser, on doors, on the dashboard of my car, and anywhere I lingered for more than five seconds. As I stood, I might read the verse aloud and let its truth sink into my mind and soul.

I read the verses while I prepared dinner, washed dishes, dried my hair, or got ready for work. I spoke them aloud when my shame was triggered. I thought of them while I drove to work or ran errands.

At first I read the verses and scoffed at the words. They sounded hopeful but unavailable to me personally. When I tired of reviewing the same ones over and over, I looked up new verses and posted them again, hoping the truths might become real to me. Romans 12:2 says I am transformed by the renewing of my mind. I needed to tell myself the truth before I was ready to believe it.

After I had focused on these Scriptures for months, I began to feel the wrestling of my spirit deep within me. What if I believed what these words said? What if I risked trusting these truths? I was afraid to believe them. I knew they had to be true because God doesn't lie. I didn't know how to lay hold of them for me. How would the words get through the imaginary brick wall of self-protection around my heart?

The verses rotated through my home, my car, and my workplace for two years. Because I read them often, I began to know many of them by heart. The ones I memorized as a child took on new meaning.

We love him, because he first loved us. (1 John 4:19 KJV)
For the Lord is good and his love endures forever;
> his faithfulness continues through all generations. (Ps.
> 100:5)

Opening My Heart

Nothing in me knew how to feel loved. I had lived so long with a wall around my heart, feeling ineligible for good things. I didn't know what to do with these verses from God's Word. If things were going to change, I needed to open my heart to it. If I risked removing a few imaginary bricks of the wall guarding my heart and let in the love I read about in these verses, I might feel that love. I might experience it.

One ordinary day, I stood by my refrigerator and read Jeremiah 31:3 slowly, as I had often done: "I have loved you with an everlasting love; I have drawn you with loving-kindness." I recited the words while I stood at the counter dicing vegetables on the wooden cutting board that pulled out like a drawer from my 1950s kitchen cabinets. I felt a resistance to believe the words of God's love.

It was as if God gently spoke the words aloud to me, waiting for me to remove some of the bricks in the walls of my heart, saying, "Louise, I love you with an everlasting love. Will you risk opening your mind to believe it and your heart to receive it?"

I felt the tension in my chest and shoulders relax. I found myself removing some of the bricks in the wall around my heart, and I let His love in. I *felt* it. Not for long, because I put the bricks back in, but it had penetrated my heart for those few seconds. I kept at this practice of risking, sometimes every day, and sometimes not. As often as I took some of the bricks in my wall down, I felt it. I experienced God's love. God never forced Himself on me. He waited for me to be willing. He stood near me with open hands until I could take the gift that had been offered.

Each time I relaxed my shoulders and removed a few more imaginary bricks around my heart, the lies of my shame lost strength. Little by little, a day at a time, my wall had more holes in it, and I experienced God's love. When painful circumstances happened, I put some of the bricks back in place, but they didn't stay long. I liked the freedom I felt and the lightness I experienced in my spirit when the bricks came down.

Receiving His Love

In this process, the unexpected happened. The love and acceptance of God became a heart experience, and I grew in confidence and contentment. Although many more places in my heart and mind needed healing, as much as I knew how to at the time, I received God's love for me.

I didn't recognize the change in myself right away, but soon I did. I didn't feel as envious of others and their stations in life. I could feel genuine joy when friends experienced the good things I had not yet experienced. I didn't feel shame and anger when I walked back into my modest home after I had been in someone else's well-furnished home. I could feel excitement when someone else achieved what I had not yet achieved. The greatest miracle was that I could begin to let my children and husband grow and mature at their own pace. I didn't need them to be perfect for me to feel good about myself.

I started to recognize the genuine strengths I could offer others. My influence was no longer limited to my talents and abilities. It was about my heart, what Christ in me wanted to do through those capacities. I had been uniquely created with a purpose in revealing God's heart to others through my specific design. I was not better or less than anyone. Life wasn't about a rating scale or a competition. It was about joyfully living out His purpose for me. I could have confidence in who I was, knowing that I, along with everyone else, have something distinct to offer the world.

It's not a race. It's a celebration. If I remained living a simple life, I knew I would like it, even love it. As I stopped comparing and trusted God with His purpose for me, I could have fun and let my life be about others and not about myself. It energized me to live like this.

God wants to free us from shame and the comparison that comes with it. He longs for us to trust Him so we can live in confidence and contentment. As we do this, we find our greatest fulfillment in giving our lives away for His glory.

Chapter 15

Ashes to Beauty

The junior-high-camp declaration of my desire to be used by God for His kingdom purposes remained the cry of my heart. I understood that I didn't need to compete with others to find contentment. I still dreamed of being in full-time ministry but couldn't foresee it happening. How could anything positive come from the travesty of my past?

During the intense first years of processing my childhood, I sat with Rick as we waited for other team members to arrive for a meeting. I poured out my complaint to him.

"All I do is work on the issues from my childhood. I don't think I will ever have the ministry expression my heart longs for. I feel disqualified. I fear I will never be healthy enough for meaningful influence."

Rick thought for a moment and then asked, "How old are you, Louise?"

"Thirty-six," I replied.

He broke out first with a grin and then a guffaw. He then said, "Louise, you're only thirty-six! You have a lifetime ahead for God to use you."

My perspective was off. I had lived my years looking at life through the veils of my shame. I didn't understand that God's work of healing in my thirties was His plan to ready me for what lay ahead. At the time it felt like a punishment I didn't deserve. Instead, it was a preparation for the calling of my life. The nitty-gritty of the daily disciplines to humble my heart and stay teachable before God and others was perhaps the most important work God had for me to do in that season. Discipline, according to Hebrews 12:11, never seems pleasant at the time, but painful. I strained at the bit, fighting God's work in me. I judged it was a discipline that should have been reserved for my abusers.

Risking Transformation

When I think of the pain of shame resulting from abuse, discipline seems a strange or even unjust part of the healing path. It is, however, a critical piece of the process. Giant steps in my emotional development were missed because of the abuse. Part of me wanted to be coddled since I hadn't experienced the nurturing I craved after the abuse. I did need comfort as I faced the enormity of what happened to me. In the process of healing, I often felt like a little girl inside. Comfort and empathy in pain is a valid need. I received tender care from Nancy, Rick, and many friends who walked alongside me as I recalled the abuse. Yet there came a time for me to grow out of that childlike state of desiring ongoing nurturing and walk into maturity. Maturity, in part, comes through discipline and risks to do what seems unpleasant.

The discipline came as I recognized my shame and chose to stand in truth instead of in the lie of what my shame told me. I had to practice trusting truth. Transformation can't happen without it. Christine Caine, in her book *Unashamed*, wrote, "This is always much easier said than done. Being set free and walking in freedom are not the same. The first was done for us by Jesus, but the second we must choose to do ourselves in his strength and by his grace."[28]

God doesn't expect us to white knuckle the discipline. None of us can recover from shame in our own strength. Christ at work in us through the Holy Spirit gives us the ability to say yes to God, opening our hands to trust Him when we want to say, "No. I don't want to learn to trust You." Philippians 2:13 says, "It is God who works in you to will and to act according to his good purpose." The indwelling Holy Spirit gives us Christ's resurrection power to choose to trust when we are afraid. God's great gift to believers in the healing journey of shame is the power He gives us to do what we cannot do on our own.

Strong Women

The shame message I received as a child regarding my strong personality included my parents' convictions about women in the church. My parents believed and touted that a strong woman, or a woman who is a leader, cannot be a godly woman.

"Godly women are quiet, unobtrusive, and should only have the spiritual gifts of mercy or helps," they instructed.

I had none of these qualities or gifts. I was not quiet and unobtrusive. Wherever I went I could not seem to stay in the shadows. I was always in front, taking charge of something. My parents' message that my design as a strong female leader made me unacceptable to God caused deep injury.

I believed all conservative evangelical churches, including mine, had the same view my parents did. At our church, women were not in positions of leadership except in cross-cultural work. I complained and gossiped to my friends about how the church takes advantage of women, only allowing them to serve in places where men didn't want to serve. My childhood experience was the foundation for my assumption about our church.

Recognizing My Leadership

A few weeks before my fortieth birthday, Rick gave me a call.

"Louise, I need to schedule a meeting with you."

Scheduling meetings was a common occurrence because of the partnerships Rick and I had in ministry together. I didn't think much of his request.

"This is not about ministry this time, Louise," he continued. "It is time we talk about you."

I knew what was coming. Rick knew me well and understood what needed to happen for me to grow.

"We have waited a long time to come to this point, but we can't avoid it any longer," he said. "Let's find a time to meet." He invited me to bring Chuck.

My stomach turned and my hands shook. I knew the time was right, but I feared what he would say.

A few days later, Chuck and I sat in his office.

Rick began, "Louise, I have often heard you say that our church does not allow women in leadership. Did you hear this from one of our elders, or is it something you have assumed?"

I stammered, having been caught in my gossip. "I . . . uh . . ." I realized then that, indeed, no one in leadership had ever said this was true. "No . . . but I don't see any women in leadership except for women in cross-cultural ministry . . . I guess it was the conclusion I drew from what I perceived."

"It isn't true," Rick replied. "All spiritual gifts, including leadership, are non-gender specific in Scripture. We would celebrate women having a role of leadership among us. If you would have asked about it, we would have told you."

I listened, feeling revealed but not scolded. We both knew my sin of gossip had been exposed, but he didn't mention it. He was more interested in ministering to my heart and teaching me than focusing on my sin.

Rick went on. "I don't think your struggle is about this church. I think the struggle is within you because of your childhood. I think you have a hard time owning what is true about you. I understand because we know what your parents told you about women in church leadership. Since you are now in an environment that allows you to be who you are and celebrates you for it, it is time you own it for yourself. I would like us to be quiet for a few minutes until you can name what is true about you."

We sat in silence for a few minutes while I wept and trembled. I knew if I admitted aloud what he asked me to own, something would break free in me, but I still feared. In a few minutes I worked up the courage to put the fingers of my right hand in the shape of an *L* and put those fingers on my forehead. I said through tears, "Okay! I admit it. I . . . am . . . . a . . . *leader*." My tears tumbled into a full sob.

In patience, Rick waited for me to come to this place of recognition of my leadership ability. His timing was wise. Then he said, "It is time for you to own it, Louise. No more of this blaming others for why you aren't released into your influence. We are not stopping you. You are the one who is stopping you. You need to fully embrace what is true about you so God can free you to live in it."

Through my tears, I nodded and said I understood what he was telling me.

He then added, "I won't say it for you. You need to say it for yourself. I think you are more than a leader. I think you know the call of God on your life is for more than being a leader, but I wouldn't be helping you if I said what you needed to own for yourself. This is about you believing God for your life."

Brené Brown, in her book *The Gift of Imperfection*, wrote, "Because true belonging only happens when we present our authentic, imperfect selves to the world, our sense of belonging can never be greater than our level of self-acceptance."[29] I needed to accept myself and what was true about me so I could experience the acceptance of God and others. In stepping into my design, I stepped into my place in the body of Christ. Having a place to belong is about relationship. It is also about having a place where your strengths and gifts are welcomed, celebrated, and released.

A few months after this meeting in Rick's office, I came on staff at our church as the children's pastor.

Protection in Community

For a church or faith community to successfully help believers move from the identity of their past to the release of their gifts, strengths, and passions, they must practice defining one another by who they are in Christ. Still, it is critical to look at the unresolved issues that affect us. My past wasn't overlooked. It was addressed fully. If the leaders of my church would have seen only my gifts and strengths and released me because of them, my woundedness would have hindered my influence. My shame issues would have brought harm and distortion to my ministry expression.

They were right to care for me—and the effects sin had on me—before I was fully released into ministry leadership. The elders' protection of me in this revealed their wisdom and their shepherding heart for me and the people of the church. When I had matured so the shame of my past no longer defined me, I was trusted to step into the role to oversee and shepherd children's ministries. They were wise to wait until I was healthy.

In the first decades of the church, hundreds of people like me pursued Rick for pastoral care and counseling, desiring to be mentored in the truths of the new covenant life of grace. Rick's gifts in training believers were used by God to bring great strength and value to the church. He practiced 2 Timothy 2:2: "And the things you have heard me say in the presence of many witnesses entrust to reliable men who will also be qualified to teach others."

Passing the Baton

After some years into in my healing journey, I asked the elders if I could start a support group for women who had experienced childhood sexual abuse. My heart to pass on to others what God taught me helped bring purpose to the suffering. In the four years of that group's existence, Rick met monthly with my co-leader and me to train us in shepherding these brave women. He mentored us in how to deal with challenging scenarios. He taught us how to help the women learn God's truth when they had experienced great harm. He invested in us so we would have a firm grip on helping others heal from the effects of sin.

My pastor's wisdom to release me to lead and at the same time train us as facilitators of the group produced great fruit in the lives of the women who participated. This was an important lesson for me. He didn't control. He shepherded. His umbrella of protection gave me tools to serve well. I was grateful for Rick's supervision and generous sharing of his experience and insight into the journey of healing from the destruction of sin.

At the time, I could not have guessed that God had a broader plan. Through those meetings, this supervision was used by God to prepare me to walk alongside scores of men and women in the years that followed. What I learned from the training would extend past that group and into the lives of many others.

Just before I came on staff, Rick stepped down from his role and joined a few others to start a new ministry outside of our church. We were excited for him and his team to pass on the truths of grace in a wider influence. We wanted others to walk in the freedom in Christ we had learned from him.

A few years into my stint as children's pastor, Rick stopped by my office. After a brief chat, he leaned back in his chair and spoke these words to me. "The baton has been passed to you, Louise. You know that, right?"

I sunk a little deeper into my chair, feeling the weight of his words. I nodded and quietly responded, "Yes, I think I do."

He then instructed, "Handle it wisely, my friend." With that, he stood and left my office.

I don't recall anything else from that day except Rick's words to me and the seriousness with which he spoke. More and more people were coming to me for mentoring in ministry leadership and for pastoral counseling. The brokenness of my past and the long journey to healing had given me compassion, understanding, and desire to help others trust God to break the power of shame in them. Rick's and Nancy's investments gave me the methodology for the process. With the support of the elders, I carved out a portion of my work week to meet one on one with people in need.

Rick remained available to me for supervision through the decades that followed. He gave me insight to handle the most complex situations and confirmed when I believed professionals needed to be brought in. His investment in me didn't end when we stopped meeting one on one to process my childhood. His investment continues to this day.

There is incredible beauty in this plan of God. "Praise be to the God and Father of our Lord Jesus Christ, the Father of compassion and the God of all comfort, who comforts us in all our troubles, so that we can comfort those in any trouble with the comfort we ourselves have received from God. For just as the sufferings of Christ flow over into our lives, so also through Christ our comfort overflows" (2 Cor. 1:3–5).

In the redemption of our brokenness, He creates beauty and uses it for good. God took me in my shame and sin and transformed what was brokenness into life-giving strength. He gave me "a crown of beauty instead of ashes" (Isa. 61:3). All for Him and for His kingdom.

Chapter 16

Fear to Trust

Shame is a vulnerable state. The uncloaking nature of shame produces fear. In shame we fear our flaws will be discovered and, as a result, we will be unloved and disrespected. A fear-based person can often be a shame-based person. Like me.

I feared many things for the first four decades of my life. Chief among them was my fear of failure. It is most often how my shame presents itself still today. Perfectionism and control, two of my familiar fig leaf strategies, were my attempts at dealing with that fear of failure. As I matured in Christ, I wanted to be rid of these patterns. I repented of them, but they were deep seated within me, and I needed an act of God to help me to practice living out that repentance. Because He loves me and is committed to my growth and healing, God provided that learning opportunity for me.

Children's Ministries

For thirty years, I had the great privilege of ministering to children as their teacher, pastor, mentor, counselor, and friend. I love kids. They make me laugh, delight my heart, encourage me, keep me young, and stretch my faith. Children's ministries is one of the most challenging ministries in a church. To minister to children well, you need trained, envisioned volunteers—and lots of them. Every week. Every Sunday. Every year.

During the six years I served as the children's pastor, we had no permanent church facility and met in a school. We had to set up and tear down each week, transforming middle school classrooms into spaces for babies, preschoolers, and elementary-aged children to play and learn about Jesus. All this was to happen without disturbing any of the equipment or supplies in the rooms. The principal who initially made the contract with us to meet in the school told his teachers they would receive a portion of our rent money for their classrooms, which made our presence palatable to them. Right after we signed the rental agreement with the school and sold our old church property, that principal resigned. The new principal had not been a part of the agreement and, for unknown reasons, decided the rent money would not be allocated to the teachers. As a result, the teachers did not want us in their classrooms, which created a stressful experience every week.

This challenging situation was the perfect storm God used to engage with me about my fear of failure. He longed for me to be free to rely on Him instead of on my driven perfectionism. While at the school, no matter how hard I tried, no matter our attention to detail, the teachers at the school were not pleased with our efforts. Their lives were miserable because of "the church." Their classrooms were no longer theirs because they had to share them with "the church," and they believed that "the church" was careless and took advantage of them. I had been a classroom teacher myself, so I understood some of the frustration of having to share.

I came early and stayed late every Sunday, making sure every classroom was in the order the teachers left it on Friday. We made intricate maps of every room that we followed to a T, with placement of desks and other equipment. We covered the teacher's desks with sheets so children weren't tempted to touch anything. We met monthly with the principal and other representatives from the school to hear any complaints of details we missed. No matter what the set-up and tear-down teams, the faithful children's ministers, and I did, it wasn't enough. The teachers wanted us gone. The fact we couldn't leave until we found a new facility wasn't their concern. My futile efforts to please them wore me out.

If that weren't enough to make a driven perfectionist give up, other challenges crept into my children's ministries world. I had delightful kids I shepherded along with their supportive parents. I also had a dynamite leadership team and hundreds of tireless sacrificial teachers, leaders, and support workers who gave time and energy to honor the children of our church. It humbles me to remember their loyalty to Jesus, to the kids, and to me.

As any leader in children's ministries can attest, attempting to have all your ducks in a row while recruiting volunteers can be an exercise in futility. It is simply not possible to have full personnel in place all the time. If the hundreds of people needed yearly for ministry teams are set, it is inevitable that one or two or ten or twenty of them will have a change in circumstances and need to step off their team. A children's pastor can never sit back and relax. Because the work is never done.

My Ideal Children's Pastor Self

In that season at the school, God schooled me. I couldn't achieve perfection. Children's ministries was not going to have the seamless functioning I wanted it to have. Every week of the year, my ducks weren't in a row and children's ministries wasn't perfect. At least that was how I evaluated it. Since 100 percent is the only acceptable score for a perfectionist, my rating turned up as failure on a regular basis. Each long Sunday, sometimes in the 110-degree heat of Phoenix, I cared for the children and those who ministered to them, helped with setting up and tearing down all the equipment, and made sure everything was in place in each classroom before I left the facility. I then went home, downed a quart or more of water and four pain relievers, and lay on the bed in my darkened room out of sheer exhaustion.

In my office during the week, I sat with fear and shame, believing I wasn't a perfect children's pastor. My ideal self—my ideal children's pastor self—would have full teams in place at all times, the school happy with our presence, and joyful children learning about life in Jesus. My aim for perfection was unreachable. Impossible, even. I was afraid. I feared failure. If I failed, everyone could see I was not my ideal self, and they would not respect me. I would not be valued.

My fear drove me at times to be unhealthy in my leadership. I wasn't as patient or gracious as my heart longed to be. On occasion I was edgy with those I served. This was not my desire. I yearned to be a safe and trusted leader. How could that change? What would alleviate my fear of failure?

A verse kept returning to my mind: "I sought the Lord, and he answered me; he delivered me from all my fears" (Ps. 34:4). Oh, how I ached for that to become my reality. I prayed, "God, let this verse become true for me. Please deliver me from my fear of failure. I don't know how You will do it, but please have Your way in me. Please liberate me from my fears. I want to be a leader like others were for me. Fear doesn't reign in their lives like it does in me. Please rescue me, God."

Shame in Disguise

As I spent time with God, I began to understand that the fear was my shame in disguise. The panic I carried was from the shame that still held power in me. I feared that if I failed, my relational needs would go unmet. If I were unsuccessful and everyone lost respect for me, it meant I would never amount to anything. The notion of being rejected for not measuring up terrified me. Shame kept my vision obscured.

Ultimately, I feared because I didn't trust God. I didn't trust God to take care of me. I didn't trust God to give me significance. I didn't trust God to come through to supply my relational needs or the needs in children's ministries. After all, I was the one who set up countless one-on-one recruiting meetings to share the vision of discipling children. I was the one who needed to think of a last-minute substitute when team members couldn't fill in for each other. I was the one to sit across the table from an angry teacher at the school and listen to their complaints. God wasn't doing any of that for me. He wasn't a genie who would give me my three wishes on command. I had to do the work. Where was He in that? No wonder I feared. I felt alone and burdened by the endless tasks.

Day after day, week after week, God began to unleash me from my fears. Rarely a Sunday went as planned. Yet, if I took an objective look at children's ministries without the veils of my shame and fear, it wasn't a failure. It was one of the strongest ministries in our church at the time. We had hundreds of volunteers who had been well trained to understand that the ministry was not childcare—it was discipleship. Every child was equal in importance to the adults. The children learned deep things of God from an early age and were treated with utmost respect and care. We had strong teams that worked together, fully committed to the children.

God was powerfully answering my prayers for the children of our fellowship above and beyond what I could have asked or imagined. When I focused on His provision instead of the perfection my shame craved, I could trust and rest. The veils of shame made my focus blurry, creating uneasiness and anxiety. I needed a clear focus with a firm foundation under my feet to move forward without fear.

I quoted a verse when my shame and fear arose: "When I am afraid, I will trust in you" (Ps. 56:3). The answer to my fear and shame was trust. I needed to trust what was true rather than what the fuzzy vision of my shame told me. My shame told me I was alone, and it was up to me to make children's ministries succeed. The truth is that God is our provider, and I could look to Him to meet our needs. Psalm 20 spoke to our challenging circumstances while in that facility. I longed to stand strong in God's promises found within the passage.

> May the Lord answer you when you are in distress;
>> may the name of the God of Jacob protect you.
> May he send you help from the sanctuary
>> and grant you support from Zion.
> May he remember all your sacrifices
>> and accept your burnt offerings. Selah
> May he give you the desire of your heart
>> and make all your plans succeed.
> We will shout for joy when you are victorious
>> and will lift up our banners in the name of our God.
> May the Lord grant all your requests.
> Now I know that the Lord saves his anointed;
>> he answers him from his holy heaven
>> with the saving power of his right hand.
> Some trust in chariots and some in horses,
>> but we trust in the name of the Lord our God.
> They are brought to their knees and fall,
>> but we rise up and stand firm.
> O Lord, save the king!
>> Answer us when we call! (Ps. 20)

Trusting God

I brought this psalm to my children's ministries leadership team, and we agreed to ask God to provide for us. For twenty-four hours, my dedicated team joined me to fast and pray through these and other verses. We then committed to fast and pray every Friday morning for a year, bringing our requests to God for His provision. It was a tough season for us in the school, yet God met us in those prayers. We were confident He heard our cries.

In those twelve months, it seemed God revealed every place where I didn't trust Him in my role. I recognized when I took matters into my own hands. It became obvious when I lacked faith in His power. He brought to light my resentment and disillusionment. He showed me the futility of my self-effort and the hollowness of my cynicism. If I could trust Him instead of trying to figure it all out myself, it would be a lot less work.

As I began to lean on God instead of myself, I learned that when I needed a volunteer, I could ask God who I should call. Instead of combing through the church directory for my own idea of who might be available, I waited to hear God speak to me. As I waited, a name or two came to mind. Often it was the name of someone I wouldn't have thought of on my own. I then called and shared the opportunity to serve, explaining the vision and beauty of what we attempted to do in each classroom. Sometimes the person agreed to consider it, and other times they didn't. In time I found it didn't matter. I moved from recruiting out of fear and shame to recruiting out of trust in God's provision. My tension decreased, and my hope increased.

In this new practice, I understood more of what was going on in me before. I discovered I had an agenda with God.

"If God really loved me, He would . . ."

"If God is who He says He is, He would . . ."

"If God gives the victory, then it should look like . . ."

I realized I wanted God to come through for me in the way I wanted. I didn't understand that having my ducks in a row wasn't going to lift my fear and shame. It only delays the fear and shame from returning until tomorrow or next week when everything is again not in place.

God provided for us in children's ministries even when I believed I was the one to create the teams. In my self-focused effort, I missed God's faithful provisional gifts. He wanted me to trust Him to meet the needs in His way. God didn't force me to ask for His help. When I was ready to release my striving and wait for Him, He revealed His power. The responsibility was not all on my shoulders. He was and is our strength and our provider.

Celebrating His Faithfulness

Fasting and praying were not our efforts to appease God or work hard so He might grant us something in return. Fasting and praying were about spending time with our loving Father. In His presence we remembered His goodness and faithfulness. We thanked Him for the miracle of the hundreds of people who served our children with full hearts. We were grateful for this facility, as challenging as it was, that met our need to have a place for children to be loved and wooed to God's heart.

At the start of that year, we invited our church to join us in prayer for our kids and this ministry. When the year ended, we celebrated together. We had enough children's ministers for each week, like manna in the desert. I stood at the front of the room, an old and funky middle school auditorium, and proclaimed the words in Psalm 20:

> May the Lord answer you when you are in distress;
>> may the name of the God of Jacob protect you.
> May he send you help from the sanctuary
>> and grant you support from Zion.
> May he remember all your sacrifices
>> and accept your burnt offerings. Selah
> May he give you the desire of your heart
>> and make all your plans succeed.
> We will shout for joy when you are victorious
>> and will lift up our banners in the name of our God.

May the Lord grant all your requests. (vv. 1–5)

God had won the victory, not because of our perfection, but because He is perfect and faithful to His name. We created small paper banners taped to straws, and on those paper flags were God's names: Jehovah Jireh, Almighty God, All-Sufficient One, Elohim, Redeemer, Savior. Ushers distributed banners to every person in the auditorium. The children came marching down the aisles waving the pennants above their heads. We shouted, "Hosanna to the King of Kings! Hosanna! Hosanna!" in one voice. We lifted the banners high.

There were many teary eyes that day, including mine. God won the victory by supplying our needs in children's ministries. Greater still, He moved my heart from fear and shame to trust. I learned that I am enough in Him. He answered my prayer with Psalm 34:4: "I sought the Lord, and he answered me; he delivered me from all my fears." He heard our cries and abundantly met our needs. We marveled at His goodness to us.

Chapter 17

CONDEMNATION TO COMPASSION

As I stepped into ministry leadership and began to see redemptive fruit reaped from the pain of my history, I was heartened. My identity was no longer in what happened to me but about who I was in Christ. My children were young, and I parented in a healthier way. I lost weight and felt beautiful for the first time in my life. A few kind men at work and church even told me so. We went on a family vacation, which was a dream fulfilled for me. It seemed my past was behind me and a promising future lie ahead. I thought I had turned a corner and life would be wonderful and happy. I smiled more often, laughed, and believed I had something to offer. I passionately pursued Bible study and ministry. Life felt lighter, and I experienced less shame.

Two dynamics impacted me in those years. The first was the journey to grow in humility and grace. I loved the freedom and hope cultivated in me as I believed more of God's truth and love. Each time I chose faith instead of fear and shame, I matured, gaining strength and skill to live in healthy relationships with God and others. The second dynamic was the old way of self-protective survival. With one hand I held onto Jesus, and the other hand held my familiar fig leaves. Progress was slow but steady, and change was evident. I was encouraged because I knew how far I had come.

If Only

My dream was to fully heal from the effects of my childhood abuse so my family wouldn't be harmed by the aftermath. Within this dream, I discovered I had a subconscious plan to redeem my story by becoming the parent I deemed mine should have been. If I could be an ideal parent, my girls would have what I wished I would have had. I would have created good out of the evil I experienced by parenting exactly the opposite of my mother and father. This aim produced an unobtainable standard of excellence for me.

Chuck questioned me, "When will the bar be high enough, Louise?" He daily witnessed me pressing to achieve an unblemished performance, then chiding myself when I didn't hit the mark. He recognized the toll my drivenness took on me and our family.

What I didn't understand until my girls were older is that it takes many years to heal from the severe abuse I experienced. It took longer than I hoped. I grew and mended, but areas of my life still required ongoing healing. In the years before the healing process began and in the slow growth afterward, the woundedness in me injured my daughters. I didn't want this to be so. I hated that I often reacted in old ways. I couldn't hurry the process of growth, and this left me feeling helpless.

As I faced the reality of how my brokenness affected my children, I felt overwhelmed with guilt and self-condemnation. The very thing I had not wanted to do, I did. I hadn't abused my children as my parents did me, but I wounded my children. I didn't have words for it until then, but I set myself up for failure. I wanted to be a perfect parent so I didn't hurt my children, and in trying, I hurt them. Because I wasn't giving grace to myself, I couldn't give grace to them.

Regret consumed me. If only I started my healing journey before I had children. If only I healed faster so I was more stable for them. If only I could have stayed home with them instead of working so I could give all my energy to them. If only I repented earlier so I didn't injure their hearts as I did. If only I learned before I did how my criticism affected them. If only, if only. The words of regret.

Judge and Jury

As I grew in awareness of the effects of my shame on my daughters, I created a running tabulation of every mistake I made and the wrongs I committed against them. I believed anything less than a perfect performance on my part was damnable. My list of failures included the mistakes I made as a new mother, the times I was too emotionally exhausted to play with them, and the parenting skills I lacked because I never learned them. The list contained my sins against them, like when I was unfairly critical, spanked in anger, or blamed them for my behavior. My self-contemptuous modeling as a female and my displays of rage toward their father also made the list. It was extensive—pages and pages long.

As both judge and jury, I found myself guilty on all counts and lived in self-condemnation. The guilt I suffered was tied to my shame. My shame told me that only someone as deficient as me would hurt their children as I hurt mine. I had no idea how to give myself grace as a mother. In viewing myself through the veils of my shame, I condemned what I perceived. My shame interpreted my mistakes as complete failure. I told myself often that I should never have been a mother. I was too screwed up to be a mother. My girls deserved better than me. I was grief stricken.

Forgiving Myself

What confused me was that my family didn't seem to condemn me. I believed every issue in our family was my fault. I asked myself why my husband and daughters didn't see it that way. Perhaps they were in denial about it. The burden I carried was heavy, and I needed help. Chuck agreed to join me in a few counseling sessions with a Christian psychologist who had helped me years before.

As we sat in this man's office, I unloaded my struggle of the season. His conclusion revealed that the issues I mentioned were rooted in my anger toward myself. He asked Chuck if he noticed my self-condemnation.

Chuck smiled and said, "She recites her list of failures as a mother all day every day."

Surprised, the psychologist asked if it was true. I nodded. He suggested I spend some time forgiving myself. I knew he was right, and I left his office with that goal in mind.

I had learned the process of forgiveness through the journey with my parents, so I understood the steps involved. I needed to start by naming the offenses. The enumerated list of wrongs I carried in my head, I itemized on paper. No wonder I condemned myself. The record of perceived misdeeds was extensive. Not everything on the list were sins, but it didn't matter. I chronicled my offenses and perceived harms: accidents, mistakes, things I didn't know I judged I *should* know, and my blatant wrongs. Recording the list didn't take long since I had rehearsed the inventory for years.

A conflict went on in me. I knew God didn't condemn me. I was the one who condemned myself. Whose judgment would I submit to: God's or mine? I pondered on 1 John 3:19–20: "This then is how we know that we belong to the truth, and how we set our hearts at rest in his presence whenever our hearts condemn us. For God is greater than our hearts, and he knows everything." God knows everything I ever did wrong as a mother, and He did not condemn me. Jesus took that condemnation for me on the cross, bearing God's wrath so I could be free. Yet I wasn't living in the truth of that promise.

I had strived to be perfect so I didn't suffer pain, specifically the heartache of my errors as a mother. I didn't know how to trust God with the consequences that came from my mistakes and sins. In my head, I knew God didn't condemn me, but in my heart, I didn't trust His provision. I prayed and cried out to God, asking for His help.

His Smile of Joy

During that summer, I swam laps in my backyard pool, trying to work out the energy created by the shame and grief of my perceived failures. It was an especially challenging workout because I sobbed as I turned each lap. When I couldn't sustain the weeping and the simultaneous swimming, I stopped at the deep end of the pool, pulled myself up on the ledge and cried out loud, "Have mercy on me, O God. Have mercy on me."

What surprised me as my feet dangled in the water was to hear from God in His still small voice, "Finally." Not in anger or disgust. Not in condemnation. I could feel His smile of joy. In that moment I realized I tried to get everything right as a mother in my own strength. I hadn't trusted God to do the work through me. He saw me push myself to a frazzle in the process. He allowed me to come to the end of myself and ask for His help. God patiently waited for me to receive what He had given me all along. In facing the limitations of my humanity, I understood my need for Him.

There was nothing I could do, no matter how hard I tried, to heal myself from what happened to me and how it affected me. I labored for years to do the impossible. I had not fully trusted Christ to do the work in me. In some measure, I tried to do it myself and was unable. I needed God's mercy. I needed His grace.

When I cried out, He showered His mercy upon me. I felt it wash over me like a warm blanket. I felt His compassion for my human limitations and my sin. I felt forgiven. I felt His forgiveness that was already given to me. I knew it was not because of anything I had done to earn it, but because of who He is, how He loves, and because of Jesus.

Romans 8:1 says, "Therefore, there is now no condemnation for those who are in Christ Jesus." I knew it before in my head, but at that moment in the pool, I knew it in my heart. The truth went from my head to my heart because I trusted it. I let go of self-protection and let God, maybe for the first time ever, protect my heart as a mother. Brennan Manning, in his book *A Glimpse of Jesus: Stranger to Self-Hatred*, wrote, "The first step in liberation from self-hatred is to move from the darkness of self-delusion into the daylight of God's truth."[30] Embracing my imperfections freed me to cling to the truth of God's grace. I was not superhuman and was certain to continue to make mistakes. I needed God to work through me to be the mother I wanted to be. His limitless power was available to depend on each day.

Ashes of Release

Soon after the encounter with God in the pool, I set out to finish the process of forgiving myself. I drove to a nearby park with my Bible, the pages of my perceived failures, and a book of matches. I sat on a bench under a shady tree while soccer practice went on behind me. I read through my list slowly. I opened my Bible to Isaiah 53, remembering the sacrifice of Jesus on the cross. Not everything on my list was a sin, but I considered it important to recall His mercy to me for everything. I then moved through my list and forgave myself for each item. I sensed His grace as I released myself from the debt I couldn't repay. I struck a match and lit the papers on fire. The sheets flickered into ashes and lifted away on the breeze.

Grace overcomes shame. God's grace comes freely to me but cost God everything: the death of His Son. This love is beyond our comprehension. Jesus took the condemnation meant for me when He became my sin on the cross. I am not condemned because He was condemned in my stead.

As I practiced believing this truth, it set my heart at rest, just as God promised in 1 John 3:19–20. God knew how many years it would take for me to heal. I was concerned as I saw the effect of my partly healed and partly unhealed self on my children, but He was at work even when I couldn't recognize it. As I began to embrace the long-term journey of healing and learned to give myself grace, I found I was much better at giving grace to others. Instead of condemning, I lived in the lightness of offering compassion and grace to people in their imperfections. Harriet Lerner, in her book *The Dance of Fear*, said, "That what we believe is most shameful and unique about ourselves is often what is most human and universal."[31]

When I am critical, I have forgotten the forgiveness and grace that is mine in Christ. I used to call myself the "Queen of Judgmentalism." Now I ask God to make me the "Giver of God's Grace." Offering compassion and hope instead of condemnation is rewarding and frees people to live with joy.

Grace to Be In Process

Recognizing I am human like everyone else changed how I parented, altered my relationships, and freed me in ministry. It is a heavy responsibility to be the judge of everyone in the world, including yourself. It is much more life giving and delightful to instead be a cheerleader and protector. When I judge, my attention is on perceived wrongs. Trusting God as the one true judge gives room to focus on encouraging what is good, building up believers in their new nature and freeing everyone to be human.

Instead of a critical comment directed toward myself or others of, "You blew it in your sin again," I can say, "This is not who you really are. Christ in you wants to love. Christ in you wants to obey." As I learned and applied this, I heard myself telling my daughters again and again through their teen and young adult years, "Everyone has room to grow. I don't want to be defined by the sins and mistakes of my past. Let's give everyone else that same grace to be in process."

My husband and daughters don't like it when I fall back into saying something self-deprecating about my parenting. My daughters say, "What does it insinuate about us if you say you are a failure as a mom?" And Chuck says, "Louise, I was there every single day of you mothering our daughters. You were a great mom. You did many things really well. Yes, you are human and you made mistakes, but you were an outstanding mother." My grown daughters tell me the same. I bask in their grace toward me.

On International Women's Day (who knew there was such a thing?), my daughter, Emily, posted these words on social media: "My mama taught me how to clean, iron, hem, love, forgive, pray, have faith, give grace, giggle, plan ahead, bargain shop, say please and thank you, have manners, how to meal prep, cut coupons, be classy, have integrity, love people, be grateful, LOVE GOD.... Wow, I could go on and on. ... THANK YOU MAMA!!!! For teaching everything about being a strong woman. I love you more than anything!!! Happy International Women's Day!!!! Louise Sedgwick"

All glory to God. All grace.

Chapter 18

MOURNING TO GLADNESS

After six years of overseeing the ministries to children at my church, I transferred to leading the ministries to adults, serving in that role for sixteen years. I delighted in partnering with many gifted and passionate men and women. Together we created avenues for our adults to experience healing from the effects of sin; grow in training and discipleship as they matured; and serve within their gifting, strengths, and interests. I went to work invigorated each day and felt deeply humbled to be entrusted with this influence.

In the beginning, my life was characterized by shame, guilt, and chronic mourning. As I healed by God's grace, this changed. My life became less about dealing with the effects of my childhood abuse and more about living in the redemption of it. Redemption, which was once only a doctrinal concept I espoused, became my life experience. Gaining confidence about my redemption in Christ was a journey. I knew that redemption meant Jesus paid the price for me to be set free from slavery to sin and its effects, but I didn't feel released. I could spout the truth that Jesus redeemed me at Calvary but had no idea how to live in it. Until I grasped His grace, the sin and the shame that came with it held me captive in my experience. I couldn't manage my pride, rage, control, and blaming because they were stronger than I was. When I learned that Jesus's ransom meant the work to set me free was finished, I could live in the gifts and promises of that redemption (1 Pet. 1:18–19).

Like every other step in the process of healing, I needed to believe by faith that redemption was mine in Christ. I needed to practice repeating the truth in my thoughts and then submit to it. I had to allow truth to penetrate my mind and heart. Years earlier, it frightened me to take down one or two bricks from the imaginary wall around my heart. As time passed and I continued to risk this vulnerability, only a few bricks remained. God earned my trust and I submitted to Him and His truth with less reservation. This freed the Holy Spirit's work in me. I didn't fight Him as much and more readily let Him have His way in me. In cooperating with the Holy Spirit's training, truth won out over the lies of my shame.

Every day, sometimes many times a day, I reminded myself that my identity was not in what was done to me nor in the damage I created through my brokenness. If I focused on the losses and the resulting grief, my past defined me. As I submitted to the Holy Spirit training me to think in a new way—this new covenant way of life in the Spirit—the mourning diminished and I stood stronger in truth. I no longer felt imprisoned. Instead of viewing myself in the mirror through the veils of my shame, I trusted His perception of me.

Gifts of Redemption

I began to revel in the gifts of my redemption. When I leaned into the truth that redemption brought me justification before God (Rom. 3:24), the shame lifted. Shame has no place in a heart made righteous. Christ's righteousness moved me from a posture of guilt and shame to a standing in holiness. That righteous and holy person was me. *Me.*

Mistake-maker me became righteous and holy through Christ. I was no longer shame itself. I was Christ in Louise.

The self-shaming thoughts instigated often by the devil himself didn't hold power in me as they once did. Satan loves it when I agree with the lie of my shame that I am worthless. He is the accuser of the brethren. He knows that I stand justified before God, but he doesn't want me to believe it. He uses shame as a tool to accuse me so I will live without joy and purpose. Through redemption I can stand firm in God's declaration about me. Satan is defeated. He has no authority in my life. I can speak truth against his lies knowing I am redeemed from the hand of the foe (Ps.107:2). What freedom it gives me to live with the certain knowledge of my standing before God!

Shame told me I was alone and unwanted. My earthly parents walked away from me, but God never will. I am chosen by God as His adopted child; I belong to Him. Through redemption I gain a place in His family (Isa. 43:1). He is my perfect parent. He will never leave me or forsake me (Heb. 13:5). This gives me security, strength, and dignity. I feel cherished, honored, and respected by Him.

In this life in Christ, I can live in confidence of who I am and who God is, trusting Him and His precepts. I don't need to fear failure or guilt for my mistakes and wrongs. I am forgiven. I know how to lean into the Spirit for help when I want to reach back to protect myself with one of my old fig leaves. Because of redemption's finished work, I can choose submission to God's ways through the Holy Spirit's enablement (Titus 2:14). Trust and obedience to God's commands banishes shame and brings self-respect.

On my hardest days when life seems cruel, I look ahead to the sinless and shame-free eternity God promises. The home I have waiting for me in heaven demonstrates my value to God. He wants to be with me eternally. I can hardly wait to stand in His presence. Jesus redeemed me from death to life in Him (Ps. 49:15).

"Praise the Lord, O my soul, and forget not all his benefits—who forgives all your sins and heals all your diseases, who redeems your life from the pit and crowns you with love and compassion" (Ps. 103:2–4). He drew me out of the pit and crowned me with His love. I believed it. I felt it. I became confident in it. If the only redemption I experience from the destruction of sin and shame in my life is living in the confidence of His love for me, it would be enough. To live fully in the knowledge and experience of the love and compassion of God is a slice of heaven on earth.

In His lavish grace, God didn't stop with healing my shame and showering me with His love. He not only liberated me *from* bondage to shame and mourning, He freed me *to* a life outside the prison. He freed me to an abundant life. He does this for all of us who learn to trust Him with our pain. He redeems the heartaches of our lives into a purpose-filled life that brings Him glory and gives us joy. He turns our mourning into gladness.

God Intends Good

In the letter I read to my parents during our attempts to reconcile, I included the words from Genesis that Joseph spoke to his brothers. Joseph's untold grief and hardship after His brothers, in their jealousy, betrayed and abandoned him could have robbed Joseph of life. Instead, Joseph healed from their sin against him by trusting and submitting himself to God, experiencing His faithfulness. When Joseph offered a restored relationship to his brothers after a long period of separation, he spoke of God's sovereignty in their sin against him. "You intended to harm me, but God intended it for good to accomplish what is now being done, the saving of many lives" (Gen. 50:20).

When I read that verse to my parents, the fruit of the redemption of their sin against me remained in the future. At the time, the destruction of the abuse seemed overwhelming. I believed God's redemption with a mustard seed of faith, which was all God needed to begin to move toward the beauty of His plan for me.

In the decades that followed, as I shared with others what God taught me through each step of my healing journey, I saw it bear fruit. It is God's truth that sets people free (John 8:32, 36) but He used me in the unique design of my person and my story to communicate that truth. It amazed me to sit with dear ones from our congregation and listen as they asked the very same questions I had asked and struggled with shame and sin in the same way that I had struggled. I rejoiced to share the beauty of redemption with them, giving them hope for a different way of life through Christ.

It humbled and blessed me to have a front row seat to watch the miracle of healing happen in countless lives throughout my years of ministry. The blessings continued as I witnessed my brothers and sisters in Christ mature in what they learned and then pass it on to others. The circular growth of believers as they heal, mature, and then give their lives away for others remains a delight to my heart.

Timothy Trust

One of the ministries formed while I oversaw adult ministries at my church was a leadership development program called Timothy Trust. Its purpose was to encourage emerging influencers in our church, training them to live out their leadership through humility and God's design. We taught that pursuing humility is a foundational step to becoming a trusted leader.

Hundreds of adults went through Timothy Trust in my years on staff. It became a benchmark spiritual maturing experience for many. My teams and I, having learned well from those who preceded us, passed on to others the scriptural principles entrusted to us (2 Tim. 2:2). Men and women were mentored and freed to ministry expression within the church and beyond.

A regular part of the curriculum is a lesson on suffering. God uses two kinds of suffering to do His work in the maturing of the believer. The first kind of suffering is the heartache that comes from the effects of living in this sinful world. Sickness, death, abuse, addiction, and broken relationships all produce real pain. It happens to believers and non-believers alike. The second kind of suffering happens only to believers and occurs when we suffer for Christ's sake. The Word tells us that if a believer allows God to have His way in them through the pain, suffering will conform them to the image of Jesus. Suffering then produces fruit in the believer that elicits trust from those they influence.

During one round of Timothy Trust, as a way of teaching the material, the leaders decided to have a panel discussion about suffering. I was one of the leaders on the panel. We gave the mentees an opportunity to ask questions of the panel members. Thoughtful questions were posed and meaningful answers given.

One questioner asked, "Was the suffering you endured worth it compared to what you see as a result?"

The auditorium quieted as we waited for a potential answer. I found myself asking for the microphone. The people of my church know my story. They know of the abuse and the aftermath of it in my life. They know the pain and loss I experienced and the shame I carried as a result. They also know how God used my suffering as an avenue to teach me truth and dependency on Him, which I shared with them through my years of teaching and mentoring.

Reflecting before I spoke, I looked at their faces, and tears welled up in my eyes. I had invested in them with a full and willing heart for years. They were dear to me. I cherished them, and they loved me in return. I surprised myself by my response.

"I hate what happened to me. I always will. But was it worth it? God is the one to decide that. I see now the perfect plan of God in what I experienced. God allowed it so I would gain what I needed to teach you. I promise you I would not have been willing to go through the discipline of learning to trust God without the suffering. I would have been content to live a life of ease, depending on myself most of the time, and God on occasion. Through the suffering of living in this sinful world and in the healing process, I was desperate for God. I needed Him. He didn't put me through the abuse to take advantage of me. He allowed the evil in my life so it could be redeemed for you. It is what He does. He is a Redeemer. I will always grieve what happened to me, but I have learned to recognize the power and beauty of the redemption of it. Do you see? He allowed me to go through the abuse . . . for you. What a privilege it is for me that He redeemed me for you."

Tears fell, tissues passed, and hearts were full of worship. Gladness abounded. The sorrows of the past paled. My mourning turned to gladness, and shame lost more power in me. There will never be happiness for the abuse or the shame that came because of it. But there can be joy for the redemption of evil for the good of many. Only Jesus could accomplish such rapture. Psalm 126:5–6 was realized for me that day: "Those who sow in tears will reap with songs of joy. He who goes out weeping, carrying seed to sow, will return with songs of joy, carrying sheaves with him."

Chapter 19

INSULTS AND LABELS TO IDENTITY IN CHRIST

Our culture has an enormous lack of awareness of the dynamic of shame. We live in a world filled with mockery, bullying, cursing, and name-calling. Out of shame, we shame others, and they shame us in return. When someone defines us with words of contempt, the words cut deep. The stabbing penetrates because our shame lie agrees with them. Our shame lie says we are worthless, unlovable, and incompetent. The bully has discovered *and named* what we attempted to hide. They judge our abilities or lack thereof, our appearance, our differences, our personalities, or whatever is deemed to be deficient. In our shame, we fear that the insults and labels are true.

Adults and children can tear the heart out of their peers through these labels, words, and actions. These derisions can stick to us like permanently affixed name tags. We can be left out, ignored, pushed around, bullied, and abused. Names like Dummy, Loser, Fag, Slut, Worthless, Fat, Bitch, Prick, or Ho called out by other children at school and even by friends, family members, teachers, and coaches can leave a sting that poisons the soul. Coworkers, bosses, neighbors, church members, and even complete strangers give labels we remember for the rest of our lives. Left unaddressed, these words erode our hearts and minds as only evil can do.

The Power of Words

While looking for descriptors of the experience of contemptuous name-calling, I discovered the word *execrate*, which means, "to stab with words."[32] I have been execrated, and, regretfully, I have execrated others. The apostle James understood this when he wrote, "All kinds of animals, birds, reptiles and creatures of the sea are being tamed and have been tamed by man, but no man can tame the tongue. It is a restless evil, full of deadly poison. With the tongue we praise our Lord and Father, and with it we curse men, who have been made in God's likeness. Out of the same mouth come praise and cursing" (3:7–10).

In my staff role at church, men often came to my office to receive pastoral counseling. I listened to painful memories of when their "not enough" messages were born. The insults and labels from their youth carry destructive power decades later. Locker room comparisons, bullying for artistic sensitivities, and losses in sports and academics destroyed their confidence. Sexual abuse by peers or those in authority confused and shamed them. Overwhelmed teachers mocked and scorned young men struggling with undiagnosed learning differences, sending a message of incompetence. Fathers' passivity, neglect, or outright words of contempt left sons alone, without direction and hope. Mothers took out their men issues on their sons. I witnessed the effect these words and experiences had on my dear brothers in Christ, and it broke my heart.

I also heard scores of women share their grief over shame messages spoken aloud or words left unsaid that stung just as deeply: name-calling and contemptuous words that were believed. Women scorned for having too large or not enough curves and laughed at for their awkward attempts to be noticed. They were told they had nothing to offer or were only valuable if they allowed themselves to be used. They had been given numerous messages except the ones they longed for: that they were capable and beautiful, worthy to be cherished and honored for who they are. They were then left to pick up the pieces and find a way to be loved.

Words are powerful. They can build up or tear down. Bessel A. Van der Kolk in his excellent book about the effects of trauma, *The Body Keeps the Score*, said, "We remember insults and injuries best: The adrenaline that we secrete to defend against potential threats helps to engrave those incidents into our minds. Even if the content of the remark fades, our dislike for the person who made it usually persists."[33] We spew back words or thoughts of contempt on our shamers for what they exposed in us. If they were once safe people, they are no longer so. We avoid them as if we were in physical danger around them.

Mockery's Motivation

We know shaming words harm, yet mockery and bullying pervade many environments. What would motivate this contemptuous name-calling? When I don't accept my own weaknesses, my shame is ignited when I experience weakness in others. Another's frailty reminds me of my own, and I lack empathy. For many years, when I encountered a person who displayed haughtiness, I would think with contempt, *They're so arrogant,* as if I were superior to them. My judgment revealed my own shame and guilt. In remorse, I recall my conceit toward those who sinned in ways I wasn't tempted to sin. I understand now that this pridefulness was contempt in disguise. I didn't know how to give myself grace and thus belittled others. We label, condemn, and pronounce an identity, all in an attempt to keep the weakness of the other from touching our shame.

Responses to Insults

Mocking and bullying words received from others add to the pile of evidence for our shame. Without dependence on Jesus for healing, we, as men and women, make vain attempts to deal with the scorn. When men are told in subtle or direct ways that they are not worthy of respect, it confirms their shame statement of, "I don't have what it takes." They then live in a never-ending pursuit of respect, or they give up and passively take whatever crumbs may fall along their path. Women, when mocked, are given a subtle or direct message that they are unworthy of love and value. Without fully trusting Jesus, the women's shame statement, "I am not worthy to be loved or cherished," turns into a lifetime of begging, demanding, or victimization.

Another approach we may take to an affront is to attempt to prove the insults and labels wrong. Instead of standing in the truth of who we are and forgiving the insult and our offender, we may scheme ways to publicly exonerate ourselves of the barb. In this plan, our motivation is often contempt for our accusers. This only results in bitterness and loss, with the label still affixed.

Danger in Owning the Label

Until we learn how to release the labels and insults of our past, we will live with them embedded in our being, like an unremovable tattoo. The label becomes our identity. We become used to it, and it starts to feel comfortable, even though it brings us emotional pain. We think, *I am the incapable one. Everyone expects it of me. I am the weak one. I am the ugly and unwanted one. I am dumb. I am the loser, the failure. Therefore I don't have to try. I don't have to take responsibility for growth and maturing. If I own this label, I know what to do, and I know my place.*

Risking a new way of seeing ourselves and a new way of doing life can feel scary. It is unknown, and we don't know the roadmap out of the old identity. In his book *Shame and Grace*, Lewis Smedes noted, "Some of us are so hooked into shame that we are afraid we would be lonely without it. We have lived with it for so long that it has become part of our consciousness, part of ourselves, part of our being. If we lost our shame, we would not recognize ourselves. We feel toward our shame the way a person who has been in prison for forty years feels about his cell: he longs to be out of it and yet is frightened to leave it. The bad things we know often feel safer than the good things we do not know."[34]

God's gift of creating us in His image is lost to us when we own the insults spoken by others or ourselves. Insults and labels bring a contemptuous focus on the perceived weaknesses of our humanity, which gives shame power in us. Being made in His image gives us dignity and worth. Author and Christian leader, Christine Caine, wrote about this in her book *Unashamed*. She said, "You and I were created to reflect God's image. Do you know what that makes you and me? Not shame-bearers, but image-bearers of God himself. We were not designed to bear shame."[35]

Offering Grace

Our human weaknesses and limitations give no one permission to speak unkindly to us. Nor does the hurt, irritation, and even extra work that others' weaknesses produce give us permission to speak shaming words to them. We are called to be full of grace toward one another. Colossians says, "But now you must rid yourselves of all such things as these: anger, rage, malice, slander, and filthy language from your lips. . . . Therefore, as God's chosen people, holy and dearly loved, clothe yourselves with compassion, kindness, humility, gentleness and patience. Bear with each other and forgive whatever grievance you may have against one another. Forgive as the Lord forgave you" (3:8, 12–13).

A willingness to grow in self-reflection demonstrates humility. When judgmental, name-calling thoughts about another person come to mind, I must ask myself some questions. Understanding what is going on within helps me depend on the Holy Spirit's maturing work in me. I can respond out of my new nature, offering grace instead of contempt.

What is it about the weakness of this person that triggers shame in me?

What is it about their vulnerability that bothers me?

Do I struggle in the same way they do?

Am I afraid of their weakness because it reminds me of my own frailty?

Do I feel less than around them because they have strengths I lack?

Am I putting them down to make us even?

Applying this same process to my words of self-shame is another important step in my growth. When I find myself thinking, *Idiot!* after I make a mistake, I need to stop and think it through. *Hmm . . . I have just called myself a name. Why did I do that? I made a mistake, and I am frustrated about that. This mistake cost me time and effort, and now I am behind schedule and have to redo the work. But I am not an idiot. I am an intelligent woman who is capable of making mistakes.* In this way, I affirm what is true about me. I need to give myself the same grace God has given me.

We are all so human. It is why I cherish Psalm 103:14: "For he knows how we are formed, he remembers that we are dust." Offering grace keeps us on level ground in front of the cross, the dwelling place for those in healthy shame.

Put to the Test

A few summers ago I visited an old friend whom I hadn't seen in several years. While there, my confidence in who I am in Christ was put to the test. As we sat on her front porch chatting, I noticed a guardedness in her toward me. I asked if something was amiss in our relationship.

She sat quiet for a minute and then responded. "Yes. There is a problem in our relationship. The problem is you. You, Louise, are a narcissist."

I was stunned. I was confused. I was hurt. Though numbed by her words, I wanted to respond well. I asked her what I had done that brought her to that conclusion. She cited a few examples of what I had said or done. In her perception, she viewed my motive in those experiences as profoundly selfish.

In maturity and humility, I knew I should look for the kernel of truth in every criticism. I examined my heart to see if there was any validity to her accusation. I tried to be as honest as I could with myself and with her. In every situation she mentioned, I knew my motive was not what she judged it to be.

I responded that I know I can be selfish, and in my younger years I was arrogant and judgmental. I asked for her forgiveness for how I had hurt and sinned against her, naming specific examples of my wrong. I told her I loved her and didn't ever want her to feel dismissed or overlooked when we were together.

She received my apology but insisted I admit I was the narcissist she believed me to be. I told her I would pray and think about it, asking the Holy Spirit to reveal what was true. I continued, that though I can be selfish, I didn't think, in general, this label was accurate about me. This angered her, and we left the conversation with the accusation still on the table.

Afterward, I couldn't shake her words. Was what she said true of me? Am I a narcissist? Am I blind to how I affect people? Is this what everyone thinks of me, and am I just now learning of it? Am I really that self-absorbed? I couldn't think straight. I cried at her accusation and at the shame of the possibility it was true. I stayed up most of the night thinking and praying, asking the Holy Spirit to reveal anything in me that could be narcissistic.

Affirming Friends

I came back home to Phoenix and shared the accusation with my closest friends, the ones who do life with me every day and know me well, including the sins I struggle with. It is my regular practice to bring my sin into the light with trusted friends, those who will protect me in it. They remind me who I am so I live out of that truth rather than my shame.

I asked these close friends, "Is it true? Am I a narcissist, and you are too nice to tell me?"

Each woman responded first in shock at what I reported and shared words of empathy for the hurt of the allegation. My dear friends then affirmed me with what they know to be true after years of doing life up close and personal with me. They did this because they understand the importance of affirmation. Affirmation is not flattery, which is overpraising. Affirmation is truth telling with the intent to build up. Affirmation does not puff up. It humbles. It is an accurate portrayal of what is true about the person being affirmed so they remember who they are when they have forgotten.

I can still remember the tone of my friends' voices and the look in their eyes as they ministered to my heart after I had been judged. Their affirming words humbled me. They did not make me proud. As they affirmed, the shame of the barb lifted from my heart.

Affirmation brings healing to our shame. Affirmation declares what is true about us in our strengths. Affirmation stands against the message our shame tells us about our unworthiness for respect and love. It moves the focus of our eyes from our pile of evidence for our shame to our dignity and who we are in Christ. Affirmation is one of the most powerful gifts of an accepting environment. In healthy relationships, we encourage the best in each other without denying the places that need growth. We need each other for this healing. Healing from shame cannot happen in isolation.

A New Identity

My friends also reminded me of who I am in Christ: justified, forgiven, and redeemed. Because Jesus died and rose again for us, our identity doesn't have to be in the labels and insults given to us. For those who believe, our identity is in Christ Himself. He dwells within us by the Holy Spirit. Bringing Him the cruel words spoken to us out of sin and shame—and leaving them at the cross—is an important step in living out our identity in Him. At the cross we can forgive our offenders, remembering what Jesus did to forgive us. We then lay down the insults and pick up the identity He has given us instead. We are saints of God, His adopted children, His friends, His beloved ones. Now and forever.

Our identity is not the curse words or mockery we received from accusers. Our identity is not in our sin or the sin done to us. Our identity is in Jesus Christ. Galatians 2:20 says, "I have been crucified with Christ and I no longer live, but Christ lives in me. The life I live in the body, I live by faith in the Son of God, who loved me and gave himself for me." What He says about us is the truth, even when the lies of our shame-infused labels would like us to believe otherwise. Through Jesus, we are loved and valued, accepted and enough, known and embraced. We are who He says we are.

Chapter 20

Despair to Hope

While writing this book, the unthinkable happened at the church where I was on staff for twenty-two years. Complex leadership issues existed that resulted in the dismissal and resignation of key staff members. The aftereffects of the losses were hurt, feelings of betrayal, and finger-pointing. Then misunderstanding, gossip, defensiveness, relational breakdown, and shock that something like this could happen among us. Leadership dysfunction went on in other churches, but not in ours, many thought.

God had significant things to teach us. An adjustment was needed in how we viewed ourselves as a body of believers. We were not above such human messiness. Even though we love and give grace well, we have as much capacity to hurt and misunderstand one another as any other church does. In the process, we lost people, perhaps even some of our reputation, and some came to a place of despair.

Are there any churches that "get it right" all the time? Is it possible to have leaders and churches that are safe and healthy? Our precious church is still healing from this painful, refining season of our history. In the months after the leadership breakdown, I chose to take a pause from writing this book to link arms with the leaders who remained in an attempt to restore trust and direction. At times it felt like our church was hanging on by a thread. During these months we hired a long-awaited lead pastor who brought steady focus on Jesus as well as sound leadership. Healing from grievous divisions can feel excruciating and slow, but relational rebuilding began.

Despairing Life Itself

I am well familiar with despair, so I understood the hopeless feeling that some experienced in this leadership crisis. The great apostle Paul went through his own strained time and shared about it as he wrote to the Corinthian church: "We do not want you to be uninformed, brothers, about the hardships we suffered in the province of Asia. We were under great pressure, far beyond our ability to endure, so that we despaired even of life" (2 Cor. 1:8). Life can be full of tension.

When we don't know how to cope with disappointments, betrayals, failures, and hardships, and when there are no foreseeable changes in overwhelming situations we face, we can feel hopeless. Like the apostle Paul and his companions, we can despair of life itself. When life is challenging and we view our experiences through a veil of shame, we can conclude we are doomed to an existence of joyless struggle. God has not seen fit to relieve our suffering because we are unworthy of happiness. Or we blame others for our misery. If they would do what they should do, we wouldn't live in this agony.

Looking at life through a veil of shame distorts everything, including our understanding of God. Shame resides in our flesh and is a crafty tool in Satan's arsenal to attempt to keep us from seeing God accurately. If the Evil One can distract us from seeing God's glory and grace, we will miss the joy and freedom that come from confidence in His delight in us. Despair keeps us from the authentic, abundant life He designed for us.

Ideal World

One of the inevitabilities of trying to keep up the image of the ideal self is that we don't only want to be an ideal person, we want our world to be ideal. We want life to turn out as we desire, and we have a subconscious or conscious agenda for that ideal. This plan creates expectations we often don't know exist until they go unmet. Instead of a healthy response of, "I'm disappointed life didn't go as I hoped," we are undone. We become filled with despair, not knowing how to go on without our shattered dream, or we rage at whoever or whatever has blocked our goal. In shame and despair, we believe God has let us down. In contempt, we become God's judge, believing He lied to us about His goodness. We can wrestle in our thoughts with God for years, especially when our circumstances remain unchanged and our dreams and ideals persist.

Some of the struggle with despair has to do with our English usage of the word *hope*. When used as a verb, Merriam-Webster says hope is "to cherish a desire with anticipation: to want something to happen or be true."[36] To hope in this way is to have wishful thinking. There is no guarantee in such wishful thinking, even though we "wish" there were.

When we confuse this human hope with God's promise of hope, we can get ourselves into trouble that brings despair. If I am told that in Christ there is hope and my circumstances never change except to become worse, I must be careful to distinguish between human hope (wishful thinking) and the true hope found in Christ alone. If I don't make this distinction, my hope stays stuck in the desire for the ideal rather than in Him. If the ideal doesn't happen, my hope is dashed and my expectation for what God *should* have done makes me doubt His faithfulness and care, adding to the shame story I carry.

I can hope I won't be a burden to my children as I age, but I have no promise of that. My wish is for this to be true, but I don't know the future, and I may become sick someday. God knows. I can pray for years that the ideal state of my life might become a reality, even circumstances that would bring Him honor and glory, but if it doesn't happen, what then? When we pray for healing and someone dies, or slowly suffers for months and years, how do we trust Him? When we ask and wait for a loved one to come to know Jesus or return to Jesus and the years go by without their repentance, where is the hope? The trial could be about years of financial struggle, a desire for jobs, marriage, children, friendship, purposeful ministry expression, or a better living situation. Any difficulty that communicates to us that our current state is unacceptable can cause us to question God's goodness and confirm the lie in our shame.

Struggle with Hope

Viewing our unchanging situation through the veils of our shame proves to us that we are worthless and unlovable. We think, *If God really valued and cared for me, life would change and He would answer yes to my prayers.* If we don't know how to access true hope, we are left with shame and contempt toward ourselves, others, or God.

The underlying questions in our struggle with hope say, "Is God who He says He is? Is He loving, kind, fair, powerful, and true? Does He care about me and my life?" To wrestle with these questions is honest and necessary for our growth as Christians. God encourages us that we are not alone in the faith struggle. Scripture records the honest human wrestling with trust:

> O my God, I cry out by day, but you do not answer,
>> by night, and am not silent. (Ps. 22:2)
>
> Hear my prayer, O Lord,
>> listen to my cry for help;
>> be not be deaf to my weeping.
>
> For I dwell with you as an alien,
>> a stranger, as all my fathers were. (Ps. 39:12)
>
> Even when I call out or cry for help,

he shuts out my prayer. (Lam. 3:8)
How long, O Lord, must I call for help,
    but you do not listen?
Or cry out to you, "Violence!"
    but you do not save? (Hab. 1:2)

We have all been touched at some level with the reality of evil in our world. The stories with which I have been entrusted over the years have broken my heart over the depravity that exists in the human heart. We can cause grave harm to one another when we give ourselves permission to do what we want to do without thinking of how it will affect those we love.

Free Will

Yet our God gives us free will to receive or reject Him. It is the way of love. This free will, this choice to do what we want to do, can produce behavior that is outright wicked.

A few summers ago, I was privileged to go with a team from my church to the country of Bosnia-Herzegovina, a breathtaking and beautiful land filled with warm, hospitable people. I was to teach at a retreat for the women from several small evangelical churches there. These humble and strong women have persevered through great trials and the tragedies of war. Their lives are hard, and yet they honor God in all they do. I could learn much from them.

While there, our team toured a genocide museum in the capital city of Sarajevo, which told the story of the Srebrenica genocide. In July 1996, during the middle of the latest war that ravaged the land and lives of the people, the enemy's army raided the town of Srebrenica. In secret, the soldiers took men, women, and children away on buses to a remote location in the mountains and shot them dead in cold blood. It was a massacre. A genocide. They buried the bodies in a mass grave, concealing the evidence of the crime. The families in Srebrenica had no idea of the carnage but knew their family members were missing, over seven thousand people in all. The full truth was not known for almost twenty years, when the gravesite was uncovered and bodies were exhumed.

Being there in the genocide museum, seeing the evidence of the horror, brought back memories of the evil I experienced as a child. I found my thoughts turning cynical as I walked among the pictures and listened to the story as told by the woman narrating on my rented headphones. "I know this evil," I sneered. I felt the old wall around my heart creeping up.

I knew my own flesh is capable of all kinds of evil and identified with the apostle Paul, as the chief of sinners (1 Tim. 1:15). By the miracle of God's grace, I carried no contempt for the killers. We stand hand in hand in front of the cross as those guilty of nailing the Savior there. I also stood in solidarity and compassion with those who experienced the evil itself and the devastation that followed. I had lived this too. I identified with the open wound that remains in souls touched by this diabolism. I knew cynicism is an expression of anger and contempt, so I understood immediately what was happening within me. The old simmering anger mixed with shame stirred in my mind and heart.

How can a loving God allow such horror? Why didn't He stop it? And why didn't He protect those people from what surely had to have been a living hell? How in the world would their loved ones and countrymen ever be able to trust and believe God is good?

I had years of healing and opportunities for growth surrounded by people who offered me unconditional love, I had matured as a believer, and still I wrestled with these questions. What hope could I possibly give the Bosnian women? And what hope is there for those who have suffered such malevolence? Hope must be as accessible and real to everyone equally if God is the God of love that He claims to be. Or it is not hope.

I came home from Bosnia and could not shake the conflict in my soul. I was once again caught up in despair. The words of my wrestling felt insistent. *This is it. I need answers, real answers, to the hardest question. Why does a loving God allow and even ordain horrific evil that seems only to destroy?* Yes, I know suffering matures us. Yes, I know evil can be redeemed for good. We learn important life lessons through the hard times we cannot learn another way. God disciplines those He loves. But such wickedness seemed absolutely senseless to me. *What possible good could come out of this depth of evil that would justify the cost of the devastation of it? How could He be a gracious God and allow such pain?* I begged God for a valid answer. Some days and weeks went by as I scribbled letters to God in my journal filled with anger, despair, more questions, and the old fear-based shame that He might not give me an answer.

His Answer

A year after the leadership crisis happened in our church, I decided to retire. At that time I was involved in the interview process for the lead pastor role and had the privilege of working with teams who queried many qualified candidates for the job. In most every case, these men were younger than I am by decades, with energy and enthusiasm for the leadership task ahead. As I listened to their fresh and exciting ideas, I found my response was to feel tired. It was right and good to begin again with youth and vigor, but I was ready for a new season of life. I retired soon after with the people of my church beautifully honoring me in a celebration a few weeks later.

In the year that followed my retirement, I finished a few leadership commitments I began while still on staff. I helped in children's ministries and joined our women's Bible study. On one Tuesday morning, my skilled Bible study small group leader asked the women to go for a walk and spend some time with God. We were to listen for what He might say to us. We were then to come back and share what we heard, if anything, if we felt comfortable doing so.

I found myself sauntering to the prayer garden located behind the office building. I walked toward the bench positioned behind my old office window. In front of that seat, leaning against a tree, was a cross about seven feet tall. I had viewed that cross every day for years, grateful for the prayer team that built and stationed it there long ago. I parked myself on the bench and once again gazed at the wooden cross.

I silently poured out my bewilderment to Him. "God, here I am. You know my heart. You know my wrestling. You know my fears, my shame, my confusion. Please speak to me today about these hard questions regarding suffering and evil." I had no tears, no anger. Only readiness to receive His response.

Into my thoughts came His answer. "The cross is enough." That was all He spoke to me that day. In the weeks that followed, I pondered His words. I prayed, read His Word, and listened for what He might teach me. "The cross is enough." The Holy Spirit began to unravel my arguments. He revealed to me how the cross was enough.

Unguarded Surrender

The cross proves the perfect sovereignty of God. He is perfect in His justice and perfect in His love. I need both His justice and love to trust His character and heart. By His atonement, Jesus paid the penalty for the sin of this world in its wickedness, thus meting out justice for all. No one deserves this lavish grace, yet He offered Himself because of the depth of His love. He endured the cross because it is the perfect expression of both His love and His justice. The cross is the proof of His worthiness for my full trust.

In my flesh, I want a god I can control. In truth, I need a perfect Sovereign God of justice and love, even when I don't understand Him.

Grasping this truth enabled me to offer God the unguarded surrender of my heart. Attempting to put God in the box of my control kept me in a place of quiet despair. His unwillingness to be in that box was perceived by me as an accusation of shame against me, but it is His wisdom to stand in the truth of who He is. Jesus's sacrifice for me on the cross, proving His love and justice for the evil of this world, is enough.

I fell on my knees before Him. I cried, "Thank You, Father, for sending Your Son as the atoning sacrifice for my sin and the evil in this world. I, and the world, did nothing to earn these riches. You are God. I am not. You are perfect in Your sovereignty, and the cross proves it. I need Your sovereignty as God. Your plans are flawless and beyond my comprehension. I release my need to have an explanation from You for the mysteries I will never understand in my finite humanity. I confess and repent of the permission I have given myself to hold You in contempt for Your plans I disagree with, as if I knew better than You. Thank You for Your forgiveness. Thank You for freeing me to trust You from my heart."

Indeed Enough

When the object of our hope is God Himself, it is a sure thing, because He is a sure thing, even when we don't yet fully trust Him. He is who He says He is, and we are who He says we are. The good news is that He is greater than my wildest imaginings. He is God Most High, the Almighty One, our King. His love revealed at Calvary lifts our shame. The cross is indeed enough.

The suffering and evil that exist in the world pale in comparison to the gift of the cross. When Jesus was crucified, He shed His blood for the sin that created suffering and evil. When He rose again, He conquered sin and death. By faith, we can experience this victory through Him. The destruction of evil in this world is not the final chapter. Evil may win small battles today, but in eternity, it will be defeated once and for all. Christ has triumphed. The fight is already won. Our hope is not in achieving an ideal world as we would define it. Our hope is in the cross. This hope frees us from the shame inherent in despair.

God invites us to let Him lift the veils of our shame, one by one, and risk trusting Him. He desires to mature us in faith—one step at a time. Each move we make toward trusting Him takes another brick out of our wall of self-protection so we can experience His goodness that has been present every day of our lives. Shame will continue to manifest itself in this life until we die, but it no longer defines us. It has ceased to be our identity. God wants to grow us to a place of abandoned trust, where we believe Him and can open our hands to say, "Not my will, but Yours be done." This openhearted posture is the ultimate picture of lifted shame.

As we humble our hearts and grow in trust, we live more in the freedom of unguarded surrender to His love. Jesus paid the price for the sin of the world so we could experience an abundant life without fig leaves, veils, and an imaginary brick wall of self-protection. He died for our real selves, to set us free to love and be loved. When we live in this unguarded abandon before Him, we turn our faces toward Him and bask in His grace. This is a life lifted from shame.

> I sought the Lord, and he answered me;
> > he delivered me from all my fears.
> Those who look to him are radiant;
> > their faces are never covered with shame. (Ps. 34:4–5)

Acknowledgments

This book is the fruit of relationship. It could not have been written without the investment, support, encouragement, and love of many. I have never met Dan Allendar or Brennan Manning, but their teaching and books impacted my understanding of shame and trust. I am grateful for their influence. Bill Thrall and Nancy Dodd showed me Jesus through their love and protection, which changed my life. The people of Open Door Fellowship Church cared for me, believed in me, and trusted me to serve among them. I am forever shaped by the grace of Jesus that I experienced in their midst. Lori Hardin and Bruce McNicol encouraged me that I might have something to say. I would not have risked writing a book without their confidence in Christ in me. Kaye Schneider gently and patiently tutored me in the craft of writing. I am indebted to her for many hours of Zoom meetings. Georgia Nickele, Bill Thrall, Mark Huey, and Bruce McNicol gave invaluable feedback to the manuscript. With skill, grace, expertise, and kindness, my editor, Jenne Acevedo, helped make this a stronger book. In the process, she became my friend.

I am grateful to all whose financial gifts enabled this book to come to print. Their investment humbled and blessed me. The prayer team who covered me through the various stages of the process includes Beth Baker; Lyle and Margee Beardslee; Beckie Buchik; Pat and Vicky

Cotty; John and Sue DeForest; Sharon Denny; Nancy Dodd; Todd and Michelle Dufek; Devry and Rochelle Faddis; Buzz and Billie Filleman; Jeff, Lori, Elizabeth, and Maggie Hardin; Patti Holein; Kent and Darcy Kleven; Mark and Tracee Klink; Tom and Marcia Kuyper; Joe and Lynda Malloy; John and Arlene Mills; Larry and Shasteen Murphy; Rich and Nancy Nicoll; Jacob and Morgan Rendel; Helen Ryan; Rich and Melissa Short; Lezlie Shortsleeve; Laurie Strate; and EJay and Lori Winzeler.

My gratitude for this loving spiritual work is immeasurable. Countless others have encouraged me with a supportive word and through prayer. I am grateful for each kindness displayed. Thank you to Aunt Helen and Del for their unflagging encouragement. Deepest thanks go to my precious daughters and son-in-law, Rachel, Emily, and Nash, and to my beloved husband, Chuck, for cheering me on as I've embarked on this journey. Only they know how far I've come and how real the story is. Their forgiveness and grace mean everything to me. Their love is God's greatest gift to me in this life.

Bibliography

Allender, Dr. Dan B., and Dr. Tremper Longman III. *Cry of the Soul: How Our Emotions Reveal our Deepest Questions about God.* Colorado Springs: Navpress, 1994.

Brock, Rita Nakashima, and Gariella Lettini. *Soul Repair: Recovering from Moral Injury after War.* Boston: Beacon Press 2012.

Brown, Brené, PhD. *Daring Greatly.* New York: Gotham Books, 2012.

Everyday Power. "205 Inspiring Quotes by Mother Teresa on Kindness, Love, and Charity." Vid Buggs Jr. Last modified February 12, 2021. https://everydaypower.com/quotes-by-mother-teresa/.

Hersh, Sharon A. *Brave Hearts.* Colorado Springs: WaterBrook Press, 2000.

Johnston, Nicole. "Shame Cycle." Accessed February 2017. thehappinesstree.wordpress.com.

Lewis, Helen Block. *Shame and Guilt in Neurosis.* New York: International Universities Press, 1971.

Mellody, Pia. *Facing Codependence* CD3.

Mellody, Pia, with Andrea Wells Miller and J. Keith Miller. *Facing Codependence: What It Is, Where It Comes from, How It Sabotages Our Lives*. New York: Harper and Row Publishers, 1989.

Moore, Beth. *So Long, Insecurity: You've Been a Bad Friend to Us*. Carol Stream, Illinois: Tyndale House Publishers, Inc., 2010.

Northrup, Christiane, MD. "6 Steps to Release Shame and Finally Cultivate Self-Worth: How We Sabotage Our Self-worth with Shame." Accessed November 2, 2016. http:www.drnorthrup.com/self-worth-release-shame.

Rainey, Dennis and Barbara. *Building Your Mate's Self-Esteem*. San Bernadino, California: Here's Life Publishers, 1986.

Sampson, Aubrey. *Overcomer: Breaking Down the Walls of Shame and Rebuilding Your Soul*. Grand Rapids: Zondervan, 2015.

Endnotes

1   Robert S. McGee, *The Complete Search for Significance* (Houston, Texas: Rapha Publishing, 1994), 108.

2   John Bradshaw, *Healing the Shame that Binds You* (Deerfield Beach, Florida: Health Communications Inc., 1988), viii.

3   William Cloke, "Rage, Shame, and the Death of Love: Finding Stone-Musings, Monographs, and Monologues," Finding Stone, http://finding.stone.com (removed from website), 6.

4   Michael Lewis, *Shame: The Exposed Self* (New York: Free Press, 1995), 30–31.

5   David A. Seamands, *Healing for Damaged Emotions* (Wheaton, Illinois: Victor Books, 1981), 28.

6   Bill Tell, *Lay It Down* (Colorado Springs: NavPress, 2015), 177.

7   Tell, *Lay It Down*, 182.

8   Dr. Dan B. Allender, *The Wounded Heart: Hope for Adult Victims of Childhood Sexual Abuse* (Colorado Springs: NavPress, 1990), 55.

9   Allender, *The Wounded Heart*, 206.

10 Lewis, *Shame*, 6–7.

11 "Famous Quotes by Vince Lombardi," Vince Lombardi, accessed April 2, 2021, http://www.vincelombardi.com/quotes.html.

12 Brennan Manning, *A Glimpse of Jesus: The Stranger to Self-Hatred* (New York: Harper Collins Publishers, Inc., 2003), 134.

13 McGee, *The Complete Search for Significance*, 29.

14 Sandra D. Wilson, PhD, *Released from Shame: Moving Beyond the Pain of the Past*, Revised Edition (Downers Grove, Illinois: IVP Books, 2002), 144.

15 Bill Thrall, Bruce McNicol, and John Lynch, *Behind the Mask: Reversing the Process of Unresolved Life Issues* (Phoenix, Arizona: Leadership Catalyst, Inc., 2005), 53.

16 Dale and Juanita Ryan, *Rooted in God's Love: Meditations on Biblical Texts for People in Recovery* (Brea, California: Christian Recovery International, 2007), 242.

17 Seamands, *Healing for Damaged Emotions*, 98–99.

18 Lewis B. Smedes, *Shame and Grace: Healing the Shame We Don't Deserve* (New York: Harper Collins Publishers, 1993), 141.

19 Horatio Spafford, "It Is Well with My Soul," Phillip Bliss, composer (1873).

20 Larry Crabb, *Connecting: Healing for Ourselves and Our Relationships* (Nashville: Word Publishing, 1997), 92.

21   Manning, *A Glimpse of Jesus*, 9.

22   Nancy Stiehler Thurston, PsyD, "When 'Perfect Fear Casts Out All Love': Christian Perspectives on the Assessment and Treatment of Shame," (Academic Paper, Graduate School of Psychology, Fuller Theological Seminary, 1994), 6. George Fox University Digital Commons, Faculty Publications - Doctor of Psychology (PsyD) Program, accessed January 6, 2021, https://digitalcommons.georgefox.edu/gscp_fac/119.

23   Thrall, McNicol, and Lynch, *Behind the Mask*, 48–49.

24   "Steps," Adult Children of Alcoholics World Service Organization, accessed May 1, 2020, https://adultchildren.org/literature/steps/.

25   Merle A. Fossum and Marilyn J. Mason, *Facing Shame: Families in Recovery* (New York: W. W. Norton & Company, 1986), 31.

26   Harriet Lerner, PhD, *The Dance of Fear* (New York: Hope Collins Publishers, Inc., 2004), 109.

27   Lerner, *The Dance of Fear*, 176.

28   Christine Caine, *Unashamed* (Grand Rapids: Zondervan, 2016), 83.

29   Brené Brown, PhD, *The Gift of Imperfection* (Center City, Minnesota: Hazelden Publishing, 2010), 26.

30   Manning, *A Glimpse of Jesus*, 88.

31   Lerner, *The Dance of Fear*, 127.

32   "Execrate," Bible Hub, accessed March 29, 2021, https://bibleapps.com/e/execrate.htm.

LIFTED FROM SHAME: TRAUMA TO REDEMPTION

33   Bessel van der Kolk, MD, *The Body Keeps the Score* (New York: Penguin Books, 2014), 176.

34   Smedes, *Shame and Grace*, 41.

35   Caine, *Unashamed*, 33.

36   "Hope," Merriam-Webster, accessed April 2, 2021, https://www.merriam-webster.com/dictionary/hope.